Roadmap
to the
Virginia SOL
EOC English: Writing

educators.princetonreview.com

Roadmap
to the Virginia SOL
EOC English: Writing

by
Gloria Levine

Random House, Inc.
New York

www.randomhouse.com/princetonreview

This workbook was written by The Princeton Review, one of the nation's leaders in test preparation. The Princeton Review helps millions of students every year prepare for standardized assessments of all kinds. The Princeton Review offers the best way to help students excel on standardized tests.

The Princeton Review is not affiliated with Princeton University or Educational Testing Service.

Princeton Review Publishing, L.L.C.
160 Varick Street, 12th Floor
New York, NY 10013

E-mail: textbook@review.com

Published in the United States by Random House, Inc., New York.

ISBN 0-375-76445-3

Editor: David Knauer
Series Editor: Russell Kahn
Design Director: Tina McMaster
Development Editor: Sherine Gilmour
Art Director: Neil McMahon
Production Coordinator: Alexandra Morrill
Production Editor: Diahl Ballard

Manufactured in the United States of America

10 9 8 7 6 5 4 3 2 1

First Edition

ABOUT THE AUTHOR

After graduation from Mount Holyoke College, Gloria Levine received a master's degree in education from the University of California at Berkeley. She has taught grades 6–12 and has written several test-prep books on getting ready for the GED and the PSAT. Currently she lives Potomac, Maryland, with her husband, daughter, and son, and two computer-loving cats.

CONTENTS

INTRODUCTION

THE END-OF-COURSE EXAMS

The end of what? Well, it's not *the* end. The End-of-Course (EOC) exams are only the final exams for certain "core" courses offered at your school. The Virginia Department of Education (VDOE) has decided that there are certain skills that it wants you to have when you graduate high school. Therefore, in order to receive a diploma, you must pass six EOC exams. EOC exams are given in the core subjects: English, math, science, and history and social science. These exams evaluate not only what you have learned, but also how well your school has taught its students.

WHAT EXACTLY IS AN SOL?

You've probably heard the EOC exams referred to as the "SOL tests." SOL stands for Standards of Learning, which is simply the name for the specific set of skills that the VDOE has earmarked for each core subject.

For example, the Standards of Learning state that a student should be able to organize ideas in writing. So, rather than just taking your English teacher's word for it, the VDOE has drawn up its own English exam to make sure you can, in fact, organize ideas in writing (among other skills).

> **TIP:** If you want to know more about the VDOE standards, try its Web site www.pen.k12.va.us/VDOE.

If you're feeling a little nervous, don't sweat it. This book is going to ensure that you have mastered every skill that the VDOE expects you to know for the EOC English: Writing test. It will give you practice questions and explain the ins and outs of the test, and it will explain how many questions you need to get right and how many SOL exams you need to pass in order to receive your diploma. In short, you've purchased the only guide to the EOC English: Writing exam you'll ever need. Congratulations for thinking ahead!

WHO IS THE PRINCETON REVIEW?

The Princeton Review is one of the world's leaders in test preparation. We've been preparing students for standardized tests since 1981 and have helped millions reach their academic and testing goals. Through our courses, books, and online services, we offer strategy and advice on the SAT, PSAT, SAT IIs, and the TerraNova, just to name a few. The Princeton Review has created nearly twenty books to help Virginia students with their SOL exams.

WE HAVE THE INSIDE SCOOP

The EOC English: Writing exam is not immune to strategy and preparation. This book includes all of the information about the exam you'll need to do well. The Princeton Review has been looking at standardized tests like the EOC English: Writing exam for years, and we'll share our special techniques to approaching standardized tests and English questions so you'll have every possible opportunity to score your best on this exam.

> **TIP:** We have made sure that every skill listed by the Standards of Learning is reviewed and practiced in this book.

One of the biggest obstacles for students in standardized testing is test anxiety. Taking the EOC exams with your diploma on the line can create stressful conditions. In order to reduce stress and prepare you for this exam, we've dedicated countless hours of research to help you do well on the EOC English: Writing exam. In addition, we've written two practice tests to help you realistically evaluate your skills.

HOW IS THIS BOOK ORGANIZED?

This book has two primary purposes. First, we will familiarize you with the structure of the exam and recommend the soundest test-taking strategies to maximize your score.

Second, we want to make sure that you're familiar with the raw material of the exam—the actual writing concepts that must be mastered to do well on the exam. We will focus on exactly how the Virginia EOC exam tests your writing skills so you will know what to expect on exam day.

This introduction includes useful information about the EOC English: Writing exam and other EOC exams you take. Lesson 1 includes test-taking strategies and techniques that are useful for the EOC English: Writing exam and any other writing test you take. Lessons 2–11 review all of the English concepts listed in the Virginia Standards of Learning for English: Writing. The concepts in these lessons are the same ones that are tested by the EOC English: Writing exam.

The book also includes two complete practice exams with answer keys and explanations so that you can assess your skills under exam conditions. After you've worked through this book, there will be no surprises when you take the actual EOC English: Writing test.

WHAT DO THE SOL EXAMS MEAN FOR GRADUATION?

This is a big question, and you should be clear on this before you proceed to the finer points of how to succeed on this test.

Virginia high school students must pass six of twelve possible EOC exams in order to graduate and receive a Standard Diploma. But if you aren't satisfied with a Standard Diploma, there's also an Advanced Studies Diploma, which requires that you pass nine of the twelve EOC exams.

Students in Virginia **must** pass both EOC exams in English in order to earn a Standard Diploma or an Advanced Studies Diploma.

There are two Virginia SOL EOC exams in English: one in Writing and one in Reading, Literature, and Research.

If you want more information about an Advanced Studies Diploma, speak to a guidance counselor, teacher, or administrator at your school.

FREQUENTLY ASKED QUESTIONS

- **What Does the Test Look Like?**
  The EOC English: Writing exam tests two major skill sets called "Reporting Categories." Each evaluates specific English concepts and skills. Later in the book we will review all the specific skills you'll need to master to succeed on the test. If you want to peek at them now, you can check out the VDOE Web site at www.pen.k12.va.us.

There are forty-four multiple-choice questions on the SOL End-of-Course English: Writing exam. The questions break down according to Reporting Categories in the following way:

Questions	Number of Questions	Points per Reporting Category
Multiple Choice	30	16 Planning, Composing, Revising
Editing	14	14 Editing
Writing Prompt	12	16 Planning, Composing, Revising
		8 Editing
Total Number of Scored Questions:		**50**
Field-Test Items:		**14**
Total Number of Questions:		**45**
Total Number of Possible Points:		**54**

- **What is a Field-Test Item?**
  A field-test item is an experimental question that does not count toward your final score. Because you have no way of knowing which multiple-choice questions are field-test items and which ones count toward your score, answer every question as if it counts toward your score. The test writers use students' performance on field-test items to determine whether they've written good questions to use on future exams.

- **What is a Passing Score?**
  You need about 37 out of 54 points to pass the EOC English: Writing exam. There are forty-four multiple-choice questions and one writing prompt on the exam, but fourteen of them are field-test items that do not count toward your score. These fourteen multiple-choice questions are mixed in with the thirty scored multiple-choice questions, so you won't be able to tell which questions really count as you take the test. Do yourself a favor and answer **all** the questions as if they count toward your final score.

LESSONS

LESSON 1
STRUCTURE AND STRATEGIES

In the Introduction, we gave an overview of Virginia's Standards of Learning tests. Because you're reading this particular book, your main concern is the EOC English: Writing exam, so let's get down to business and zoom in for a close-up on that exam. In this lesson, we'll tell you exactly which writing skills are tested, and how they're scored. We'll show you what the exam looks like, how it's formatted and organized, and how it is scored. And we'll show you what you'll need to do your best on this exam by filling up your "SOL Toolbox" with techniques you can use on the exam.

IN A NUTSHELL

The English: Writing exam has two parts. The first part contains thirty multiple-choice questions that count (plus fourteen of those "field-test" items we mentioned in the Introduction that don't count). These multiple-choice questions are based on compositions drafted by fictional students in response to particular writing tasks. Each question presents four choices including only one that is correct. On the second part of the exam, called the "direct-writing component," there is a topic (or "prompt") for a written composition.

WHAT'S TESTED?

As you may recall from the Introduction, all the EOC exams are lined up with that list of learning goals known as the SOL (Standards of Learning). Specifically, the EOC English: Writing exam covers the knowledge and skills specified in the writing category of the Virginia Standards of Learning for ninth through eleventh grades.

This means that the EOC exams test what you learned during the school year. If you actually look at the Virginia Standards of Learning, you'll find that the writing skills are all organized under one of two groups (called "reporting categories").

- "Plan, Compose, and Revise in a Variety of Forms for a Variety of Purposes"

- "Edit for Correct Use of Language, Capitalization, Punctuation, and Spelling"

In this book, we will focus *only* on what the EOC exam will test. We will review those two basic "reporting categories" and the skills and content that you will be tested on in each category. That review will include the following content areas:

- **Writing Process:** You will need to be well-versed in specific steps in order to answer both the multiple-choice and writing sections correctly. We will review all the stages you go through before, during, and after writing your rough draft.

- **Grammar and Usage:** Certain multiple-choice questions—as well as the composition component—require you to recognize proper grammar and make the best word choices. This will include your ability to use verbs, pronouns, adjectives, and adverbs correctly. You'll also need to know the rules of standard sentence formation, such as how to avoid fragments and run-ons. We'll go over those basic rules you may have learned long ago—and we'll do our best to make them stick!

- **Spelling, Capitalization, and Punctuation:** We'll review commonly misspelled words, capitalization, and punctuation—and all the other skills the Virginia Department of Education has targeted for the writing exam.

Now that you know what the exam looks like overall and what skills are tested, let's focus on each of the two parts: multiple choice and direct writing.

MULTIPLE-CHOICE COMPONENT

The multiple-choice part of the exam may be a little different from multiple-choice tests you've taken in the past. The test makers have made up questions that reflect what students do when they write in real life. There are several scenarios that describe actual writing tasks—situations in which a fictional student writer has to compose a piece of writing for a specified audience. Following each scenario is a question about an activity the writer might do *before* drafting the piece. Here is a sample of this type of question.

Why I Would Be Good for This Job

Erin is applying for a job as a clerk at a music store. On the application is a space where she is supposed to explain why she would be a good person to hire for the job.

---

1 **Which of these would *best* help Erin get started on her application essay?**

   A Brainstorming reasons she needs to earn some money

   B Listing past jobs and experiences with music

   C Writing the rough draft of her application

   D Listing all the pieces she has learned to play on the zither

You will then be given two sections of the rough draft written by the fictional student in response to the task. Each sentence in the draft is numbered. Some questions require you to look at a sentence or two from the draft. You will be offered four possible revisions and asked to choose the one that is the best improvement on the original. Other questions might ask you to identify a sentence in the piece that should be deleted or fixed. The odd-numbered questions will have answer choices lettered **A, B, C,** and **D** and the even-numbered questions offer choices **F, G, H,** and **J**. These questions about how to revise the draft before editing won't necessarily follow the order in which sentences are found in the draft and "As it is" will never be an answer choice.

Here are the directions that might come before the first section of the draft.

Here is the first part of Erin's rough draft. Use it to answer questions 2–5.

Then comes the draft, followed by the questions. Here's a section torn from the draft plus a sample question that might appear on this part.

---

(1) Music Mania should hire me because of my sales experience and appreciation of music. (2) Having worked part-time for the past three years and having been a music-lover for a long as I can remember. (3) I feel that I would make a valuable addition to your staff.

(4) My sales experience includes work in a clothing store, a card shop, and a hardware store. (5) During my time as a clerk at Fannie's Fashions, I learned that ....

---

2 Which of these should be revised because it is *not* a complete sentence?

A 2

B 3

C 4

D 5

The second section of the rough draft contains errors in language use, punctuation, capitalization, and spelling. The directions read something like the following:

Read this next section of Erin's rough draft and answer questions 6–9. This section has groups of underlined words. The questions ask about these groups of underlined words.

Then you will see the draft with numbered sentences.

> (11) Music has always been special to me. (12) <u>I take flute, piano, and guitar lessons</u> and plan to be a music instructor someday. (13) I have a large collection of CDs and enjoy reading the music reviews in the Sunday *Washington Post*.

Questions that follow the second section of the draft will require you to look at part of a given sentence that may or may not contain an error. These questions do follow the order of the sentences in the draft and "As it is" is always an answer choice. If there is an error, there is only one and your job is to find the answer choice that corrects that error. If there is no error, don't be afraid to select "As it is." Read the following:

3   In sentence 12, how would <u>I take flute, piano, and guitar lessons</u> be correctly written?

   A   I take flute piano, and guitar lessons

   B   I take Flute, piano and guitar lessons

   C   I take flute, piano, and guitar lesson's

   D   As it is

DIRECT-WRITING COMPONENT

This is the part in which you actually have to *show* that you can write by *writing something*. Makes sense, right? You are given a prompt that is in the form of a question, an issue, or a hypothetical "what-if" situation. A sample prompt might be

In your opinion, what is the greatest challenge that teens face today?

The prompt will be followed by a "Checklist for Writers," which the test makers give you. It has several important points to keep in mind as you plan, draft, and revise your paper.

Here it is.

CHECKLIST FOR WRITERS

___I planned my paper before writing.

I revised my paper to be sure that:

___ the introduction to my paper captures the reader's attention;

___my central idea is supported with specific information and examples that will interest my reader;

___the content of my paper relates to my central idea;

___my writing is organized in a logical manner;

___my sentences are varied and read smoothly;

___my word choice develops my purpose and tone; and

___the conclusion brings my ideas together without restating.

I edited my paper to be sure that:

___correct grammar is used;

___words are capitalized when appropriate;

___sentences are constructed and punctuated correctly; and

___words are spelled correctly.

___I reviewed my paper to make sure that it accurately reflects my intentions.

Source: The Virginia Department of Education.

As mentioned in Lesson 1, you will be provided with scratch paper and a dictionary (but not a thesaurus—go figure). Writing under exam conditions isn't always fun, but some of the pressure will be lessened in this case because you can *take as much time as you need* on the direct-writing portion of the EOC.

The scorers will evaluate your writing according to how well it reflects your mastery of the three SOL skill areas, or "domains." These domains are

- composing

- written expression

- usage and mechanics

We will review these three skills areas, and we'll give you plenty of writing practice so that writing the "real thing" will be a piece of cake. We promise! Now, let's translate these "skill areas."

Composing: This is the process of organizing your ideas. Is there an introduction that captures the reader's interest? Do you support your central idea with plenty of specifics? Is your writing logically organized? Is there a conclusion that ties the ideas together? Think of the EOC exam scorers as new-house inspectors. They will only approve a well-constructed home that is built according to an orderly plan and that rests on a solid foundation with plenty of support. We'll go over how to develop that plan and how to make the grade with the "inspectors."

Written Expression: This is about how you use language. Do you communicate effectively? Do you choose precise words that create the right tone for your particular purpose and audience? Are your sentences varied? Do they read smoothly? We'll review how to do all this and more so that the test scorers will be impressed by what a "way with words" you have!

Usage and Mechanics: This skill set covers all those rules of grammar, capitalization, punctuation, and spelling that you've been learning since first grade. You may believe that what you say is far more important than how you say it, but on the EOC (and in real life), this often is not the case. Presentation (including legible handwriting) matters. We'll review how to polish your writing skills and gain total control over the language.

SCORING

As we explained in Lesson 1, the score on your English: Writing exam is calculated from the number of correct answers on the multiple-choice component, combined with the number of points earned on the direct-writing component.

A machine will score the multiple-choice section of the exam. Teachers and other professionals will score your written composition.

At least two scorers will read your writing piece. They will each come up with a score from 1 to 4 in each of three "domains" (skill areas per the SOL). Then, all of their scores are *combined*. That means if one scorer gives you a 3 in the "composing" domain and the other scorer gives you a 4, your total score in that domain is 7. In other words, you could get a score of anywhere from 2 to 8 in each domain.

> **TIP:** To review: You can earn a maximum of 30 points from the multiple-choice section, where there are 30 items that are scored (plus some "field-test" items that don't count), and a maximum of 24 points for a piece of really fine writing in response to the prompt. A passing score on the exam is 37 or higher. The highest score you can get is 54.

As we explained in the previous lesson, score points from the "composing" and "written expression" domains are assigned to one "reporting category" (Planning, Composing, and Revising), while score points from the "usage and mechanics" domain are assigned to another reporting category (Editing). If all this talk of domains and categories and separate scores sounds a little confusing, don't think too much about it. You're not the one who has to score this thing, right? Your job is just to put all your writing skills *together* and produce an effective piece of writing. We'll lead the way.

When everything's added up, you'll earn a total of somewhere between 6 and 24 points from your writing. If you've followed the Checklist for Writers that comes with your exam (and, of course, we'll go through that checklist step by step), you will have written a premium paper and earn close to 24 points for it (depending on how well your scorers agree with each other).

Scorers are given a scoring guide that tells them briefly how to judge whether a paper deserves a 1, 2, 3, or 4 in each domain. If the scorers think that you have a "reasonable" handle on things, but that your writing shows some inconsistency in all three domains, you'll earn about 18 points. If your scorers agree that your writing is pretty weak in all three areas, you'll get 12 points. If your scorers both give your writing a thumbs-down in all three areas (composing, written expression, and usage and mechanics), you'll get 6 points—and flunk the exam as a whole, no matter how well you do on the multiple-choice section. Don't worry. Work with us, and that won't happen.

YOUR SOL TOOLBOX

Throughout this book, we'll help you fill up your "SOL Toolbox." We'll give you tools to handle problems you face on the EOC exams and others. What strategies will end up in your kit?

SOL TOOL #1: PROCESS OF ELIMINATION (POE)

Try the following question:

> **In sentence 15, how would <u>the secret be to keep from guffawwing</u> be correctly written?**

You haven't the slightest idea of what *guffawwing* means and how to write the sentence correctly? Don't panic. Lucky for you, all the EOC multiple-choice questions come with four alternatives to choose from.

    F the secrit is to keep from guffawwing

    G the secrat is to keep from guffawwing

    H the secret is to keep from guffawing

    J As it is

Can you spot any answer choice that is definitely wrong? You can zap **F** and **G** right away as soon as you notice those weird spellings of *secret*. When you're editing for spelling errors, you'll need to use some gut instinct. If a word just plain looks wrong, it often is. Even if you don't know what *guffawwing* is or exactly how it's spelled, those double *w*s look wrong, don't they? When was the last time you saw a word with two *w*s in a row?

Although you may not know how to correct sentence 15 on your own, you can figure out the right answer by eliminating the choices that are wrong. You may have heard of this strategy called "Process of Elimination" (POE for short).

It is often easier to detect the wrong choices than the right ones. We suggest that you literally cross out those wrong choices first. That way, you narrow down your choices, and it is easy to see what's left. Even if you can't eliminate three out of four choices right off the bat as we did with the sample item, you still improve the odds with each choice you eliminate. It's better to make a wild guess among two or three choices than among four—and remember, you're not penalized for guessing. So, narrow down the field as much as you can and then make your best guess.

Now you have the first tool for your kit: the POE. We'll be mentioning it throughout the book because we think it is one of the most useful test-taking strategies you will ever learn. (Try it the next time you lose your keys.)

SOL Tool #2: Aggressive Guessing

Try another item.

Here is the first part of Mariana's rough draft. Use it to answer question 1.

> (1) High school is a time when kids try to express their individuality. (2) Students begin to develop their own sense of style. (3) Desperately trying both to fit in and stand out. (4) Teens are often self-conscious. (5) Many lack the confidence they need to assert themselves. (6) They use clothing and outward appearance to communicate who they are. (7) Requiring students to wear school uniforms would take away an important opportunity for self-expression. (8) I am against the new proposal to adopt these uniforms.

1 **Which of these should be revised because it *not* a complete sentence?**

    A 3

    B 5

    C 7

    D 8

You can guess that the answer is **A** before looking at your choices. When you read Mariana's draft, you may have noticed that something was wrong with sentence 3. Read it aloud to see if it makes sense as a complete sentence. It doesn't, so it's not a complete sentence. (It's a fragment, an incomplete idea that cannot stand alone as a sentence. Don't worry if you forget why—we'll go over all of that in the upcoming lessons.) It's a good guess that the answer will be the choice that says "sentence 3."

Sure enough, you look at your four choices and—BINGO—there it is, **A**. If you had carefully checked each of the sentences in the other choices *before* guessing, they might have confused you. Of course, you can't always make an aggressive guess before looking at the four alternatives. Read the example on the following page:

> **Leandro has been assigned to write a story about a new coach at his school. He wants to describe the coach's background and explain his philosophy of coaching.**

Which of these would best help Leandro get started on his story?

Well, which of these is it? You really can't guess which is the best way for Leandro to start until you've seen your options, right? Here they are.

A Watching a video of sports bloopers

B Coming up with a headline for his story

C Interviewing Coach Leandro

D Writing the first draft of his story

Now you can use POE to eliminate **A**, **B**, and **D**. The video wouldn't tell Leandro anything about the new coach. He'd need to gather the facts by talking to the coach before he drafted his story and gave it a headline.

To sum up: When you can, it's most efficient to guess aggressively what answer you are looking for, and then look for it among the choices. It's like eating at the mall. You could just go to the food court and look at all your choices and then decide what you want. But if you're hungry and want to save time and energy, you should probably decide what you want, then find the place that sells that food.

SOL Tool #3: Backsolving

Sometimes the choices themselves, not the question, should get most of your attention. In fact, you can sometimes figure out the answer by working backward, starting with the choices, even if you don't quite get the question! We'll call this strategy "Backsolving." Let's try it on this question.

In sentence 2, how would <u>last night the quarterback gedoopered</u> be correctly written?

A last night the quarterback gedooper

B last night the quarterback gedoopers

C last night the quarterback will gedooper

D As it is

Now try working first from your choices. You can cross off choices **A**, **B**, and **C** because they all contain errors you can probably spot a mile away. (We'll go over these "verb tense and agreement" errors in later lessons.)

You may not know what *gedoopering* is, but you know that you need a form of *gedooper* that goes with *last night* (past tense) and with *the quarterback* (singular). That helps you knock off the first three choices:

> *Today two* quarterbacks gedooper, but not last night—and not the one quarterback—so **A** is wrong.

> *Today* the quarterback gedoopers, but not last night—so **B** is wrong.

> *Tomorrow* the quarterback will gedooper, but not last night—so **C** is wrong.

> *Last night the quarterback gedoopered*—so **D**, *As it is,* is correct.

SOL TOOL #4: THE WRITING FRAME

While we cannot tell you exactly on what topic you will be asked to write in the writing component of the exam, we can make some predictions: It will be a question, issue, or situation of interest to students that will generate different ideas, but not anything too controversial. You will probably have to persuade your readers that your ideas about something are right.

While there is no correct answer to your prompt, you will need to make your main idea clear and support it with plenty of well-organized reasons and examples. How well you state and support your main idea will determine your score.

In Lesson 12 we will present you with an easy-to-follow "writing frame" or template that you can use for expressing your thoughts on any topic. This writing frame is an outline or pattern that will help you organize your ideas and stay focused. We will also go into a lot of detail about strategies for building your composition, and we will give you practice answering EOC exam-like prompts.

COMMONLY ASKED QUESTIONS FROM STUDENTS

Does it really matter if I get sloppy about darkening in answers and erasing mistakes?

You betcha. This exam requires you to complete a Scantron© sheet, which, as we said, is scored by a machine. That machine recognizes pencil marks. Period. It certainly can't tell that you *meant* that little pencil squiggle just outside one space to be your answer or that you *didn't mean* that half-erased pencil smudge in the other space to count.

Are they trying to trick me when "As it is" appears as the fourth choice, and it seems to be right?

Remember that about one-fourth of the questions will have the final choice as the correct answer (just because test makers like to dish out the right answers pretty equally to all four locations). Since almost half of the multiple-choice questions have "As it is" as an option, that means that there probably *will* be a few times when "As it is" will be the answer.

Can I write in the exam booklet?

Yes! The exam booklet is yours, for now. You can and should make all sorts of marks in it as you eliminate choices, notice key words, find answers in passages, and so on. And when you write your composition, you should brainstorm and definitely write and organize your ideas in the booklet. Just make sure that you neatly write your finished composition on the four pages of lined paper you are given.

GENERAL TEST-TAKING TIPS

You've heard it all before, but it's really true.

- Get a good night's sleep before the exam (but don't overdo it so you wake up feeling sluggish).

- Eat a good breakfast (but that doesn't mean steak and eggs if you're used to a breakfast bar).

- Bring at least three sharpened #2 pencils.

- Remind yourself that you are in control. You've gone through this book, you've done the practice exams, you know the exam like the back of your hand, and you are ready!

···PART II···
ANALYZING THE WRITING PROCESS

LESSON 2
PLANNING AN ESSAY

You've probably heard the phrase "writing process" in your English classes. In general, this phrase refers to the idea that good writing is done in a series of steps—not as a one-shot deal. When you sit down to do most pieces of writing, the Virginia educators think that you should go through these steps, described in the Virginia Standards, for the best results.

- Planning (prewriting and warm-up activities)

- Composing (getting ideas down on paper in rough-draft form)

- Revising (improving sentence formation and overall organization)

- Editing (correcting errors in language use, capitalization, punctuation, and spelling)

The EOC exam-writers believe that by using these writing process steps, you'll become a better writer—not only in school, but out in the "real world." That's why they've put several questions on the exam about the steps—even the one that comes *before* you start writing your draft!

In the next ten lessons, we'll walk you through writing questions that are just like what you'll find on the EOC exam, and then we'll have you practice several of your own. As you may recall from Lesson 2, there are two "reporting categories" on the exam. In this lesson, we'll practice working on those multiple-choice questions in that "Plan, Compose, and Revise" category. These are questions about what writers do before, during, and after writing the first draft—but before polishing the piece.

The polishing step—editing for grammar mistakes and proofreading for nitty-gritty mechanical errors—is covered by questions in the category, "Edit for Correct Use of Language, Capitalization, Punctuation, and Spelling." By the time you finish Lesson 12, you'll have covered both categories on the exam (and the respective SOLs). In other words, you'll be ready for anything the exam writers throw at you.

THE INSTRUCTIONS

Before we begin, let's take a moment to get a feel for what the directions on the multiple-choice section of the writing exam are like. First, you will be given a title and scenario (a brief summary of a situation in which a pretend student does some writing).

Here's a sample.

My Position on the Chewing Gum Issue

Twain has decided to write a letter to the School Board. He wants to state his position on a recent proposal that chewing-gum chewers be suspended from school.

Then you'll see a question like the following:

▶ **Which of these would *best* help Twain get started on his letter?**

  A Taking part in a debate about punishing gum chewers

  B Interviewing someone who has worked at a candy counter

  C Conducting a survey about different brands of gum

  D Observing gum-chewing behavior at a local mall

Another question might start with a scenario like the one below.

> **Tali's teacher has asked students to write a story based on any trip they've taken. Tali has decided to write about a recent school trip to the Chesapeake Bay.**
>
> **Tali made a list of events that happened on the trip. Use it to answer question 1.**
>
> 1. The Environment Club sponsored a trip to help clean up the bay.
>
> 2. On Sunday, I gathered some gloves and headed off to meet the bus.
>
> 3. Grumpy Don said that since I was early, I could help him count the trash bags.
>
> 4. Early people are sometimes considered overeager.
>
> 5. We picked up trash from the beach for six hours.
>
> 6. At the same time, I looked in vain for sharks' teeth to add to my collection.
>
> 7. While we were turning in our trash, Don called to me.
>
> 8. I thought he wanted help again, but instead he handed me something.
>
> 9. He turned away before I could thank him for the three perfect sharks' teeth.
>
> 10. The clean-up day had been rewarding in more ways than one.

Then, an exam question will follow.

▶ **Which of these is *least* relevant for Tali's list?**
F 2
G 4
H 7
J 10

Basically, this kind of question is testing your ability to think ahead and plan out a writing piece. Therefore, you will need to think about how this student got ready to write.

After one question of this "planning" sort, you will then be given a piece of the draft that the pretend student wrote, with each sentence numbered. Finally, you'll be given a second piece of the draft, another set of directions, and another set of questions. These are all questions about editing the draft for correct use of language, capitalization, punctuation, and spelling—the type of questions we'll go over in Lessons 5–8.

At the beginning of the exam, you will find four sample items with directions. Now that you know what the directions and questions look like ahead of time, you won't have to spend much time on them the day of the exam. Let's talk about how to answer writing questions of the first type—those that have to do with what you do *before* you write.

THE PLANNING STAGE

Before you actually start writing, it is important to get those creative juices flowing. It would be pretty hard to write without having anything to write about! Of course, you could plunge right in and just start writing your draft off the top of your head, or try coming up with a title first, but that's usually not such a good idea. It often leads to tangled, disorganized, and unfocused writing. Usually, it ends up as no writing at all! Prewriting activities are sort of like warm-ups before sports: well worth the time and effort to avoid later pain. Here are some prewriting activities that can help spark ideas:

BRAINSTORMING
Here you *can* just start writing out of nowhere. You can come up with as many ideas as you can and just jot them down. The idea is first just to list everything that comes to mind—without worrying at this point whether the ideas are strong or weak or in what order they should go.

CLUSTERING

Here, you start off by putting the topic in the center of a piece of paper and circling it. Then, you start jotting down ideas about that topic in bubbles around it. Then, you jot ideas about *those* ideas in clusters of bubbles around *them*. Let's say you were going to write about your personal hero. Here's how you might begin clustering ideas.

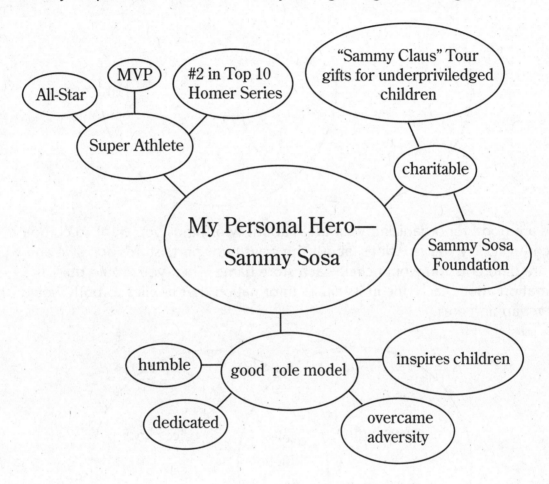

VENN DIAGRAM

You've probably seen these. They look like this.

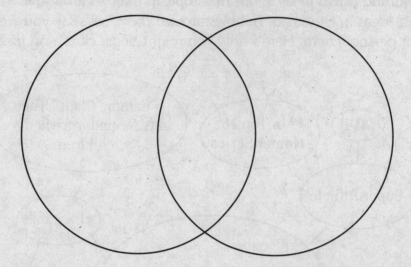

These are good for organizing your ideas about two things you want to compare and contrast. Say you're writing about the ways two sports stores are alike and ways they are different. You would circle each store name. Then you would put information about each one in its circle. Information that applies to both would go in the overlapping area.

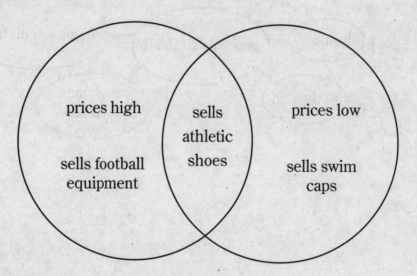

Olympic Sporting Goods   Top Dog Sports

1.   1.

2.   2.

T Chart

This is just like it sounds. You draw a big "T" on your paper and compare two things or people on several points. For example, if you're writing about whether or not you want school uniforms, you might list pros on one side and cons on the other.

For School Uniforms	Against School Uniforms
1.	1.
2.	2.

More Warm-Up Ideas

Not all warm-ups have to involve a paper and pencil. Here are a few other prewriting activities that you might do to spark ideas.

- **Do some research.** This one may sound obvious. If you're writing about the endangered black-footed ferret, you'll need to look up information from various sources—books, magazine articles, Web sites, animal experts, and so on. But you'll also need to do research before requesting information from these sources. For example, before you contact a ferret expert, you'll need to do some research to find out who these experts might be and how you can contact them.

- **Watch a video.** Videos often provide lots of background knowledge that can help you understand more about your writing topic. For example, if you're writing an English paper on the book, *The Diary of Anne Frank,* watching a video about World War II might help you analyze the book more intelligently.

- **Administer a survey.** Suppose you're writing an article about how students feel about cafeteria food or you're writing a research paper on attitudes toward the census form. An efficient way to gather information is to survey people. Ask them all the same question(s) and tally up their responses. Then you can talk about exactly how many students seem to think the tacos are delicious and whether there seems to be a trend for junk-food lovers to be cafeteria-vegetable critics.

- **Conduct an interview.** Suppose you're assigned to write a story about a relative or classmate, or about the experience of someone who has lived through the Depression? What better way to come up with details than to go to that person with questions in hand and interview him or her?

- **Do some role-playing.** This is really helpful when you are writing a story. For instance, if you're trying to show a scene in which a teenager argues with her mother, actually acting out such a scene would probably help you come up with some natural-sounding dialogue.

- **Hold a debate.** When you're asked to write a paper defending your position on something, it may be hard at first even to figure out your position! There's nothing like actually arguing about the pros and cons of something like school uniforms to help you sort out what your opinion is—and why.

- **Sit and observe.** Suppose you're writing a story about a conversation two teenagers have on a bus, or a description of how squirrels behave. Take a seat, open your ears and eyes, and you'll get plenty of details to use in your writing.

Of course, the type of prewriting activity you do has to be tied to the type of writing you are going to do. If you're going to be pitching baseballs, one type of warm-up will help; if you're going to be running a 150-yard dash, another kind is needed. Likewise, if you're writing a story about a real person's war experience, it's a good idea to interview a military veteran. On the other hand, if you're writing about a particular battle, you might want to watch a video on it first.

When you decide on a prewriting activity, choose the one that best *fits your purpose.* That means you should start out by making sure you're clear about what that purpose is. Then figure out what kind of info you need and do whatever will get you the most *usable* ideas. In other words, choose the right bait, and fish where the fish are.

On the writing exam, you will probably be asked to figure out which of four prewriting activities would best help a pretend student writer, so let's do one of these questions together.

> **Erin is feeling anxious about a take-home essay test that is due tomorrow. Her friends try to help her relax so she can write her essay.**

▶ **Which of these strategies would be the *most* likely to help Erin relax and get down to work?**

   A Suggest that she take a few slow, deep breaths

   B Offer to take her on a ten-mile hike

   C Yell at her to "Relax!"

   D Suggest that she imagine herself in the dentist's chair

Of course, **A** is the best answer. A simple thing like stopping to take a few deep breaths really does help a lot of people calm down.

If you're not quite sure what the best answer is here, now is the time to get out your SOL Toolbox and pull out your reliable Tool #1—Process of Elimination (POE).

By using POE, you can easily eliminate **C** and **D**. Yelling certainly won't help. Think of the last time someone told you to relax, in any tone, for that matter. Was it helpful? And while visualizing a *peaceful* place could be a good way to relax, imagining being in a dentist's chair is hardly relaxing at all!

What about **B**? Isn't walking supposed to be good for relaxation? Probably so, but a ten-mile hike won't leave much time for writing the essay. Erin might end up totally crashing afterward. Cross off **B**. This is an activity that doesn't fit the whole purpose, which is getting Erin relaxed and ready to write her essay.

Try these questions on your own.

Cereal A and Cereal B

Cedric has done a science fair project comparing and contrasting two brands of cereal. He needs to write a paragraph summarizing his findings.

Before writing his paragraph, Cedric made a Venn diagram. Use it to answer question 1.

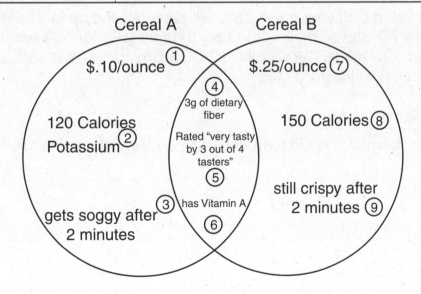

1 Which item in Cedric's Venn diagram is *least* relevant to his paragraph?

A 2

B 4

C 5

D 6

> Daniella is a tenth grader entering an online writing contest sponsored by a wildlife society; winning entries will be published in a collection of animal stories. Daniella decides that her story will be about a childhood memory of one of her pets, but she hasn't selected which one yet.

2 **Which of these would *most* help Daniella get started on her story?**

   F Making up a title for her story

   G Watching a public TV special about unusual pets

   H Listing the pets she had as a child

   J Beginning to write her first draft

Now check the answer key on page 33.

So far, we've talked about how to come up with ideas for writing. Now it's time to talk about the next planning step—organization.

ORGANIZATION

Once you have all your ideas, it's tempting to plunge right in and start writing your draft. Don't! If you do, all your good ideas will probably end up in a jumble. Instead, if you take a few minutes to think about how to order your ideas, it will be well worth the effort. Any reader—especially an EOC exam-scorer—will appreciate a writing piece that is well constructed.

The Conventional Outline

You've probably learned one old form of outlining ideas, which looks like this.

   I.

       A.

       B.

          1.

          2.

       C.

   II.

Here, roman numbers (I, II, III, IV, etc.) are used for the main ideas. Capital letters (A, B, C, etc.) are used to indicate all the parts of each main idea. Arabic numerals (1, 2, 3, 4, etc.) are used for the details to support each part. Here's an example of how Jenny might start to outline a paper she's writing about getting a driver's license in her state.

Topic: Getting a Driver's License

    I. What you need to provide when applying for a license

        A. Full name

        B. Address

        C. Proof of age and identity

            1. Birth certificate

            2. Social Security card

    II. Special requirements if you're under 18

        A. Driver's education class

        B. Provisional driver's license

    III. People who are ineligible for a license

    IV. Steps in obtaining a license

Let's try an exam question you might be asked about the outline above.

▶ **Which of these belongs under heading III in Jenny's outline?**
    F   Application, in person, at the Motor Vehicles Administration
    G   Adult cosigner of minor's application for a license
    H   U.S. government-issued passport with two photographs
    J   Individuals with revoked or suspended licenses

The main idea under III is "People who can't get licenses." So, you should be looking for the choice that describes one of these types and would fit neatly under heading III. Using POE, you can cross off **F**, since this choice—showing up in person—would clearly go under IV (Steps in obtaining a license). Get rid of **G** next, since the adult cosigner would go under II (Special requirements if you're under 18), not III. Adults who cosign teens' applications had better be people who can get licenses themselves! Throw out **H** since the passport fits under roman numeral I, letter C—something you can use to prove your age and identity when applying for a license. Now you're left with **J**, and it fits perfectly under III. People whose licenses have been taken away are among those ineligible for licenses.

Cluster Map

Instead of the old standard outline, you might see a cluster map like the one you learned about on page 25.

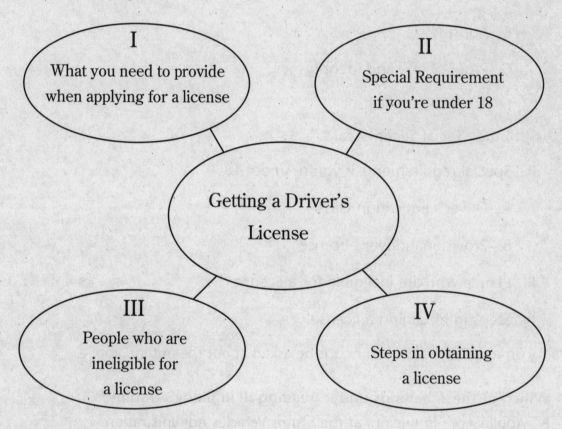

Try the following question:

3. **Which of these could properly go in bubble IV?**

   A Take a vision test

   B Habitual narcotics user

   C Suspension of minor's license on request of co-signer

   D Restriction of alcohol use

For correct answers and explanations, be sure to check the answer key below.

Let's take stock, here. You've looked at how some students have planned what they are going to write. You've practiced the types of questions you'll be asked about that prewriting stage. You've reviewed which prewriting activities are appropriate to which writing purposes (brainstorming, clustering, Venn diagrams, T charts, interviews, role-playing). And you've learned about ways to organize the main ideas and details of an essay with outlines and cluster maps. What sorts of questions come up next on the exam? Once the pretend student produces a rough draft, what will you be asked to do with it? What will you need to know?

ANSWER KEY

1. **A Planning Activity.** Detail 2 is the least relevant because it is not something that describes both cereals.

2. **H Planning Activity.** By listing pets she had as a child, Bernadette is using a prewriting activity that matches her purpose—coming up with ideas about childhood pets. Coming up with a title (F) and beginning the draft (J) are steps that come later. Watching a special about unusual pets (G) might give Bernadette lots of ideas—but not ones she could use in a story about her pet.

3. **A Planning Activity.** The question asks you to decide how ideas should be organized. Taking a vision test belongs with "Steps in obtaining a license"— bubble IV. You can use POE to get rid of the other choices because none describes steps in getting a license.

LESSON 3
COMPOSING AND REVISING AN ESSAY

The building blocks of any essay are sentences and paragraphs. The parts of a sentence relate to each other; each sentence relates to other sentences; related sentences form paragraphs; and paragraphs relate to each other to form a whole essay.

There are certain rules about how you write sentences that the EOC exam writers want to make sure you know. These are really basic rules—and you're probably sick of hearing them—but humor us for a few minutes while we review the ones the EOC exam makers think are important.

Here are topics on writing good sentences that may appear on the exam.

- Complete Sentences

- Run-ons

- Sentence Variety and Smoothness

- Parallelism

- Misplaced Modifiers

- Word Choice

The EOC Exam will cover other topics that have to do with the essay as a whole.

- Introduction

- Central Idea

- Unity and Coherence

- Conclusion

Let's spend some time on each of these.

COMPLETE SENTENCES

The Subject

Every sentence has to have a subject. The subject is *who* or *what* the sentence is mainly about. See if you can spot the subjects in the two sentences below.

    Sentence A The wrestler won the match.

    Sentence B Her tattoo is unforgettable.

Here's how to find the subject in a sentence.

1. **Find the verb (action word) in the sentence.**

2. **Ask yourself, "Who or what (performs the action of the verb)?"**

Look for the verb in Sentence A and you find *won*. Ask yourself, "Who *won*?" The wrestler *won*. The *wrestler is* the subject.

Look for the verb in Sentence B and you find *is*. Ask yourself, "What *is*?" Her tattoo *is*. Her *tattoo is* the subject.

Sentence Fragments

If the subject or verb or both are missing, you do not have a complete idea. You do not have a sentence. What you have is an error called an "incomplete sentence" or fragment. Let's look at a few examples of sentence fragments and strategies for making them complete sentences.

Incorrect: Raising both arms in victory. (Who was raising both arms?)

One way to correct the fragment is just to add a subject.

Correct: The wrestler was raising both arms in victory.

Another way is to add a subject and change the *-ing* word into a past-tense verb.

Correct: The wrestler raised both arms in victory.

Another way to correct a fragment is to elaborate on it—stretch it out, making sure the result has both a subject and a verb.

Correct: Raising both arms in victory, the wrestler pranced around the ring.

Now there is a subject (*wrestler*) and a verb (*pranced*), and you have a complete idea.

Often the fragment just needs to be connected by a comma with the ideas that follow it.

Incorrect: Raising both arms in victory. The wrestler grinned at the crowd.

Correct: Raising both arms in victory, the wrestler grinned at the crowd.

Sometimes the original fragment has a subject but lacks a verb.

Incorrect: The wrestler raising both arms in victory.

What did the wrestler, raising both arms in victory, do? One simple way to correct such a fragment is to change the *-ing* word—which is actually a noun because it describes a thing, here, a particular action—to a verb.

Correct: The wrestler raised both arms in victory.

Now let's look at how these sentence fragments might be tested on the writing exam. You might want to mark this page with a bookmark or paper clip since you will be returning to it as you work on several questions later in the lesson.

My Position on Curfews

Mike and Andres have both decided to write to their state senator about a proposal to impose a curfew on teens. Mike is against the idea, but Andres is for it.

Draft A below is Mike's rough draft of the first part of his letter. Use it to answer question 1.

Draft A: Mike's Draft

(1) Some people wanting a curfew for minors in our state. (2) They feel that a curfew would reduce crime. (3) While restricting when teenagers can be out might reduce misbehavior in urban areas, I am against imposing curfews on all teens everywhere in the state.

(4) Minors in our state are already not allowed to do certain things. (5) They are already not allowed to drive between certain hours.

(6) Adding on more to this law and still further limiting our freedom would achieve nothing. (7) It would not only create resentment but also being hard to enforce. (8) We have certain freedoms during the day, why shouldn't we have the same ones at night?

(9) Installing a curfew, teens and police would be facing unnecessary tension created by lawmakers and that would be unwise.

---

1 **Which of these should be revised because it is *not* a complete sentence?**

A 1

B 2

C 3

D 4

For the correct answer, be sure to check the answer key on page 51.

RUN-ONS

We've talked about the problem of treating an incomplete idea like a sentence and ending up with a "fragment." Another kind of sentence problem results when you have more than one complete idea running together in a sentence. This type of problem is called a "run-on."

You must separate ideas that can stand on their own. You cannot simply string them together with no punctuation—or even with a comma. You need one of these.

- period + space + capital letter

- semicolon (;)

- comma + a relationship word such as *and, but, because,* or *so*

Here are some run-ons and corrections.

Incorrect: Many people have come down with the flu, the flu shot was no guarantee.

Correct: Many people have come down with the flu. The flu shot was no guarantee.

Incorrect: The capitol dome is being restored workers are removing lead-based paint.

Correct: The capitol dome is being restored; workers are removing lead-based paint.

Incorrect: Quick fixes have been made, longer-term remedies will be needed.

Correct: Quick fixes have been made, but longer-term remedies will be needed.

Test for a Run-On

Ask yourself: Could one little period, alone, be used to separate this sentence into two complete ideas, each having a subject and a verb? Could each idea stand completely on its own as a sentence without the other? If yes, *this* is a run-on (which is a no-no) and needs to be fixed! Try the following problems:

Go back to the first part of Mike's draft on page 37. Use it to answer question 2.

2 **Which of these should be revised because it is *not* a correctly formed sentence?**

F 5

G 6

H 7

J 8

> **TIP:** Remember KISS: Keep It Short and Simple.

Check the answer key on page 51 for the correct answers.

SENTENCE VARIETY AND SMOOTHNESS

On the writing exam, you will often be given sentences that have no obvious errors, such as fragments or run-ons, but still sound awkward. They could be overly wordy or repetitious. Other times, the wording may sound choppy. In still other cases, the ideas may be out of order. Often these sentences can be tightened by deleting, rewording, and combining ideas. The best wording often expresses a complex idea while using the fewest words.

Given four choices, ask yourself: Which one doesn't trip up your tongue when you read it aloud? That's often the one that you want.

> **TIP:** Make sure your connecting words tie ideas together in the way you intended. Use the right connecting words to help say what you mean. Don't let them lead your ideas astray!

Repetitious: Grapes rolling around on supermarket floors are hazards. Hazards can result in lawsuits.

Shorter and Better: Grapes rolling around on supermarket floors are hazards that can result in lawsuits.

Awkward: Tyler does not know how to spell that word. That's why he can't look it up in a dictionary.

More Graceful: As Tyler does not know how to spell that word, he can't look it up in a dictionary.

Choppy: Chip finally cleared the dishes from his floor. He could no longer get to his bed.

Smoother: Chip finally cleared the dishes from his floor when he could no longer get to his bed.

Choppy: You can tell my parents. Don't tell my friends.

Smoother, Clearer: You can tell my parents, but don't tell my friends.

Use conjunctions (such as *and, or, but, for, since*) to combine ideas while keeping the intended meaning.

Remember:

- The words *but* and *however* signal a contrast between the ideas they link.

- Words like *so, since, because,* and *therefore* signal cause-and-effect.

- Words like *then, when, next, before,* and *after* signal when events happen in relation to each other.

Let's try the following question together:

Here is part of Tali's rough draft. Use it to answer the question that follows it.

(1) "Help Save the Bay—This Sunday" read the Environment Club flyer posted all over school. (2) Early Sunday, I put on rubber boots, grabbed some work gloves, and headed for school. (3) Don was the only one there.

(4) "You can make yourself useful by helping me count these trash bags," he grumbled.

(5) What a grump!

(6) I turned my thoughts to the day ahead. (7) I was hoping to help with the clean-up. (8) I was hoping to find some fossils for my collection.

▶ **How can sentences 7 and 8 *best* be combined without changing their meaning?**

A I was hoping to help with the clean-up and finding some fossils for my collection.

B I was help with the clean-up, I was hoping to find some fossils for my collection.

C I was hoping to help with the clean-up and to find some fossils for my collection.

D I was hoping to help with the clean-up, and for my collection, find some fossils.

Use POE to get rid of choices that contain errors or problems.

A sounds awkward and seems to have a problem with parallelism, which is a problem we'll talk more about. Tali was hoping for two things equally, so these two things should be expressed the same way: *to help and to find* not *to help and finding*. **B** is not much better because it contains a big, new problem—the run-on. **D** doesn't flow very well; the ideas seem out of order. **C** sounds just right. It's short and sweet and balanced: I was hoping *to help and to find*. **C** is the correct answer.

Try the following questions, based on Mike's draft (page 37) about his position on a curfew.

3   **How can sentences 4 and 5 *best* be combined without changing their meaning?**

   A   Minors in our state are already not allowed to do certain things, and they are already not allowed to drive between certain hours.

   B   Minors in our state are already not allowed to do certain things because they are not allowed to drive between certain hours.

   C   Already minors in our state are not allowed to drive between certain hours.

   D   Minors in our state already not being allowed to drive between certain hours.

4   **How is sentence 6 *best* rewritten?**

   F   Further limiting our freedom by adding to this law would achieve nothing.

   G   Adding on still more to this law and further limiting our freedom would achieve nothing.

   H   Adding on more to this law would limit our freedom still further and would achieve nothing at all.

   J   To add on more to this law and still further limiting our freedom would achieve nothing.

Check the correct answers by looking at the answer key on page 51.

PARALLELISM

Imagine something parallel, like train tracks. They look balanced, right? The distance between them is always the same, right? In grammar, parallelism refers to keeping like ideas in like form. Take a look at this sentence.

Incorrect: Teens discuss how to do tomorrow's homework, who's dating whom, and they talk about Saturday night's choice of movies.

Correct: Teens discuss *how to do* tomorrow's homework, *who's dating* whom, and *what movie* to see on Saturday night.

Notice that in the correct version, three similar ideas (what teens talk about) are expressed in similar form (*how, who, what*).

Look at some other examples of faulty parallelism and how to correct them:

Incorrect: Chocolate-covered raisins, cherries, and strawberries that are covered with chocolate all count as fruit.

Correct: Chocolate-covered raisins, cherries, and strawberries all count as fruit.

Three similar things (all chocolate-covered fruits) are put in similar form.

Incorrect: Phoebe learned to *play* lacrosse, *swimming*, and *the art of knitting*.

Correct: Phoebe learned to *play* lacrosse, *swim*, and *knit*.

Three similar factors (all traits Nathalie mentioned) are expressed in the same form.

Incorrect: Ross is a good athlete, but is very poor at keeping up with his studies.

Correct: Ross is a good *athlete*, but a poor *student*.

Two balanced ideas (what Ross is and what he isn't) are expressed in a similar way.

Try the following problem, based on Mike's draft (page 37):

5 How is sentence 7 *best* rewritten?

    A It would not only be creating resentment but also being hard to enforce.

    B It would not only create resentment but also be hard to enforce.

    C It would not only create resentment, it was hard to enforce.

    D It not only will create resentment but also would be hard to enforce.

Check the answer key on page 51.

MISPLACED MODIFIERS

When you modify a car you add decorations and doodads to it that change it from the plain old car it was, right? To modify means to change something or to shape it. In grammatical lingo, a modifier is a word or a group of words that change or shape another word. Let's now look at this short sentence:

Harbison's new opera opened last night.

Now, let's add a modifier to it:

Harbison's new opera, which is based on *The Great Gatsby*, opened last night.

The words between the commas certainly change and expand your understanding of the opera. The words "*which is based on* The Great Gatsby" make up the modifier. They are right where they should be, next to the word they describe (opera). Harbison's new opera is based on *The Great Gatsby.*

Now see if you can find the modifier in this sentence.

Known for her bold performances, Lorraine Liberson is wonderful as the sassy Myrtle Wilson.

Known for her bold performances is the modifier. It adds to our understanding of the subject, Lorraine Liberson. Notice how the modifier is again right next to the word it modifies—this time, coming before it and separated from it by a comma. Lorraine Liberson is known for her bold performances.

Here's a modifier that begins, as many do, with an *-ing* word.

Dragging along, the show seems as if it will never get to the final curtain.

Again, notice how the modifier—*Dragging along*—sits right next to what it modifies: the show. The show is dragging along.

So far, so good. Everything is where it should be. But sometimes the modifiers are out of place, and these "misplaced modifiers" can result in silly, or sometimes hilarious, mistakes.

Incorrect: Harbison's new opera opened last night, which is based on The *Great Gatsby.*

Was last night based on *The Great Gatsby*? No. Something is wrong here.

Incorrect: Lorraine Liberson is wonderful as the sassy Myrtle Wilson, known for her bold performances.

Myrtle isn't the one known for her bold performances, is she?

Incorrect: The show seems as if it will never get to the final curtain, dragging along.

The curtain isn't dragging along, is it?

Try the following problems, based on Mike's draft (page 37).

6 How is sentence 9 *best* rewritten?

    F Installing a curfew, teens and police would be unwisely facing unnecessary tension created by lawmakers.

    G Lawmakers would be unwise to install a curfew and create unnecessary tension between teens and police.

    H Installing a curfew, police and teens would be unwisely facing unnecessary tension created by lawmakers.

    J Creating unnecessary tension between teens and police, it would be unwise of lawmakers to install a curfew.

Check page 51 for the correct answers.

WORD CHOICE

You need to use words that convey the tone *you* want. That tone might be humorous, angry, straightforward, friendly, sarcastic. . . Can you think of others?

Consider several ways a writer might refer to you: *child, teen, juvenile, dependent, adolescent, young adult, youth, student, scholar.* Which of these words have negative associations? Would you rather someone called you a *young adult* or a *juvenile*? Suppose you're on the light side. Would you prefer that someone call you *slim* or *skinny*? What if you keep an eye on your spending? Would you feel better about being described as *someone who practices good money management* or as *someone who is cheap*?

Simply changing a few words can dramatically change the tone of two sentences that describe the same house.

> **Don't miss this cozy rambler—a fixer-upper that's perfect for the first-time home buyer!**

> **Get a load of this cramped little place—falling down so badly only someone who can't afford more would buy it.**

In many instances, it is a good idea to use *specific words* instead of settling for general ones. You'll need to ask yourself, "Which way of saying this is exactly right for what I mean?" The following chart should be helpful for finding specific words:

General Word	Specific Words
walking	swaggering, toddling, strolling
saying	whispering, yelling, joking, talking
nice	friendly, enthusiastic, sympathetic
great	entertaining, suspenseful, beautifully filmed
important	a highlight of her life, vital to world peace, crucial if we are to succeed

Here is Andres's draft of an article in favor of a teen curfew. Use it to answer question 7.

DRAFT B: Andres's Draft

(1) I think instating a curfew is a good idea to reduce crimes by and against teens. (2) Most important, it would benefit the community by keeping kids off the streets at night and out of trouble. (3) Forty percent of teens smoke marijuana on a regular basis. (4) Statistically, people between the ages of 14 and 20 are most likely to be involved in violent crimes and many of these happen at night. (5) The District of Columbia has instated a curfew and it has helped. (6) Much less important, but still worth mentioning, is that petty crimes like littering would decline if young people were not out at night tossing cans and wrappers on the streets and sidewalks. (7) Serious problems like vandalism decline when potential troublemakers are kept indoors at night.

(8) A second vital point to bear in mind is that not only are the kids committers of crimes, but they are sometimes victims. (9) By keeping youth at home and off the streets at night, they would be kept out of harm's way. (10) I would advocate enforcing a curfew in our community with the help of the local police. (11) Doesn't a curfew make sense? (12) In summary, I am for a curfew because it would cut down substantially on crimes committed both by and against teenagers.

7   How is sentence 5 *best* rewritten?

   A   The District of Columbia has instated a curfew and it has really helped.

   B   The District of Columbia has instated a curfew and it had a significant effect.

   C   The District of Columbia has instated a curfew and it had a highly significant effect on criminals.

   D   The District of Columbia has instated a curfew and it produced a moderate drop in the crime rate.

Check the answer key on page 51.

Here are some tips that will help you with questions about sentence formation. Get this down and then we'll move on to multiple-choice questions that ask you to look at the big picture—to improve a piece of writing as a whole.

HANDY TIPS ON SENTENCE FORMATION

You should remember these rules that the EOC exam-makers want to make sure you have nailed down.

- Watch out for sentences that start with *having* or *being*. These are often incomplete sentences (a.k.a."fragments").

- Be suspicious of *-ing* words. These are often used incorrectly as "misplaced modifiers."

- Be suspicious of sentences that run on and on. See if these are really two complete ideas that have been mistakenly glued together.

- KISS: Keep It Short and Simple. The best answer (among a set of four possible revisions) is often the most concise and economical. Of the choices, look at the shortest first. If it is grammatically correct and does not change the meaning of the original sentence, it is probably the correct one.

- Listen to tone of voice. Be aware of the attitude behind the words. Use words that suit the purpose.

INTRODUCTION

The introduction to any paper—whether it is an essay, a letter, a story, or something else—needs to grab the reader's attention. That can be done in several ways, which include starting with.

- an interesting anecdote or story

- a question

- an opinion that others don't hold

- a vivid description

- a statement that surprises the reader or raises a question in the reader's mind

- a clear overview of what the writer will say in the rest of the piece

Remember Andres and Mike and their letters about the proposed curfew (pages 37 and 45)? Try this question and check your answer on page 51.

8 **What is the main difference between paragraph 1 of Draft A and paragraph 1 Draft B?**

    F Draft A begins in an angry tone.

    G Draft B clearly states the writer's position in the opening sentence.

    H Draft B opens with a question to grab the reader's attention.

    J Draft A begins with an interesting anecdote.

CENTRAL IDEA

In any piece of writing, the writer needs to choose a main idea and stick to it. Every detail needs to support the main idea with some sort of example, or illustration, or explanation. Any other detail must go. All these supporting ideas form the "body" of the piece. On the EOC exam, you may be asked to weed out details that do not belong.

All you need to do is

1. Figure out the topic—the one- or two-word subject of the piece (e.g., "curfews").

2. Figure out the main idea of the piece—the main thing the writer is saying about the topic (e.g., "I am for curfews").

3. Ask yourself, "Does this detail explain the main idea?" (e.g., "Does the detail about vandalism help explain why he is for curfews?") If so, keep it. If not, it is irrelevant and needs to go.

Try this question, based on Draft B on page 45.

    9 **Which sentence contains information that is *least* relevant to Andres's argument?**

        A 3

        B 4

        C 5

        D 9

Check the answer key on page 52.

UNITY AND COHERENCE

Good writers try for one effect. They not only delete irrelevant ideas but also put the remaining ones in a logical order. Finally, they make sure that each idea is connected to the rest so that the reader can follow them—often by using connecting words called "transitions." But how do you decide on a logical order?

Time Order

If you're describing something that happened—or the steps in a certain process—it

> **TIP:** Make sure you have connected each idea in a logical order.

makes sense to put your ideas in the order in which they happened. Here are some time-order transition words: *first, later, during, after, then, finally,* and *when.*

Order of Importance

If you're trying to defend a certain position, you might arrange your ideas from most to least important—or you might reverse that, saving the most important for last. Some order-of-importance transition words are: *most important, certainly, doubtless,* and *perhaps.*

Cause and Effect

If you're explaining why something happens, or the effects of something, it makes sense to go back to the original cause or causes and explain the chain of events in order. Some cause and effect transition words are: *as a result, consequently, thus, one reason,* and *another reason.*

Comparison and Contrast

If you're comparing and contrasting two things, you might describe all the ways A is similar to B, then all the ways A is different from B. Alternatively, you might describe A completely, and then describe B completely. Some comparison/contrast transition words are: *similarly, like, likewise, in contrast,* and *on the other hand.*

Spatial Order

If you're describing the layout of a place, you might go from top to bottom, or left to right, or from the center outward. Some spatial order transition words are: *above, below, beside,* and *next to.*

The keys to answering questions about details that are out of order is to

- **Figure out the order.** Ask yourself: What do the transition words tell me about the order the writer has chosen?

- **Look for inconsistency.** Look for the detail that sticks out like a sore thumb. Is one detail out of chronological order? Are the details going from most important to least important—and suddenly a really important point pops up at the end? Do all the details—except one stuck in the middle—describe how two things or people are alike?

Try this question about Draft B on page 45 and check your answer on page 52.

10   Sentence 6 is not in the correct sequence, Sentance 6 is *best* placed directly after—

    F Sentence 2

    G Sentence 4

    H Sentence 9

    J Sentence 11

CONCLUSIONS

A good conclusion does more than just restate what you've already said. It brings your ideas together and often answers the reader's question, "So what? Why have you bothered to tell me all this?" It doesn't throw in any totally new ideas—but it may well leave the reader with food for thought about all you've said.

Try this question about Draft B on page 45 and check your answers on page 52.

11   **Which of these is a problem with sentence 12 of Draft B?**

    A It restates the first sentence.

    B It introduces a completely new idea.

    C It brings the writer's ideas together without restating.

    D It leaves the reader with an interesting question to ponder.

> **TIP:** The conclusion is the last thing a reader sees—and it may well be what the exam scorer takes away from a piece after all the rest is forgotten.

SUMMARY

Here's a list of some new tools you have acquired to help you answer the multiple-choice questions on the EOC English: Writing Exam. As you will see in Lesson 9, several of these tools will also prove handy when you write your composition.

- KISS: Keep it short and simple when you have a choice of wording. Look for the word or words that say exactly what you mean in just the right tone.

- Trim the Fat and Keep the Lean: Get rid of unnecessary words.

- Process of Elimination (POE): Eliminate any choices that create new problems like faulty parallelism or misplaced modifiers.

- Handy Rules of Sentence Structure: Spot fragments, misplaced modifiers, and run-ons.

- Create an introduction that grabs the reader's interest.

- Provide details that support your central idea and contribute to unity.

- Eliminate irrelevant details that threaten unity.

- Strengthen coherence by organizing ideas logically and connecting them with transitions.

- Close with a conclusion that does more than just summarize. Your conclusion should tell the reader why they've bothered reading your essay.

ANSWER KEY

1   **A   Identifying sentence fragments.** "Some people wanting a curfew for minors in our state" is a fragment because it lacks a subject and verb. It leaves us wondering, "What about these people who want a curfew?" All other choices are properly formed sentences. Each contains a subject and verb and expresses a complete idea.

2   **J   Identifying run-ons.** Sentence 8 is a run-on because it contains two complete ideas that could each stand alone if a period were inserted: "We have certain freedoms during the day. Why shouldn't we have the same ones at night?"

3   **C   Composing sentences that read smoothly.** Use KISS. The original sentences are overly wordy. Version **C** trims the fat by eliminating the unnecessary repetition of "are not allowed to." Notice that Backsolving works, too. Starting with the answer choices, you can cross off **A** because it is repetitious, **B** since it makes no sense (the word "because" implies a weird cause-and-effect relationship that Mike didn't intend), and **D** is a fragment.

4   **F   Composing sentences that read smoothly.** Trim the fat. Notice that **F** is the shortest, most concise answer. **G**, **H**, and **J** all contain redundant words ("adding" means "more" and "still further" is a wordier way of saying "further").

5   **B   Correcting faulty parallelism.** Use similar words to write about similar ideas: It would not only create but also be. Only choice **B** balances two simple verbs against each other to describe two similar ideas—negative effects of a curfew.

6   **G   Correcting misplaced modifiers.** Use POE to eliminate all the other choices, which contain misplaced modifiers. Both **F** and **H** make it sound as if teens and police are the ones installing a curfew. Choice **J** is weak because of where "it" appears. Since the lawmakers—not "it"—are the ones creating all this tension, they should be placed closer to that "creating...tension" modifier.

7   **D   Using specific word choice.** Choice **D** says exactly what Andres means by "helped." Cross off **A** and **B** because they are just wordier ways of saying "helped." Eliminate **C** because that is not really what Andres means. A "significant effect on criminals" is vague and could be one that results in more crime sprees!

8 G Writing the introduction. Draft B clearly states right from the get-go that Andres is for the curfew, although it takes Mike a couple of sentences before he states his position against curfews. Cross off **F** because Draft A begins in a pretty matter-of-fact tone. **H** is wrong because there is no "hook" question in Andres's opener and **J** is wrong for a similar reason: There is no interesting little story in Mike's opener to hook the reader's attention.

9 A Eliminating irrelevant detail. All the details except this one explain why Andres thinks a curfew is a good idea. He makes no connection between marijuana-smoking and a curfew, so that detail is irrelevant. On the other hand, he does make a connection between violent crimes by young people and curfews by stating that many of these crimes happen at night, so this detail is relevant.

10 H Organizing writing logically. By starting out with the transition "most important," Andres signals that he is organizing his ideas in descending order of importance—from most to least important. Sentence 6 ought to be the last detail before the conclusion because it is "Much less important."

11 A Writing effective conclusions. Andres's conclusion is weak because all it does is say exactly what he said in the beginning, in slightly different words.

LESSON 4
EDITING QUESTIONS:
NOUNS AND PRONOUNS

BRUSH UP ON YOUR GUMS!

We will need to brush up on our **GUM**s (*Grammar, Usage,* and *Mechanics*) to prepare you for the writing exam. Yikes! Nouns, verbs, adjectives, adverbs, and all that stuff? Why? Because the EOC English: Writing exam will test your ability to identify errors of sentence formation, capitalization, punctuation, and spelling.

As we discussed previously, the Virginia Department of Education has a list of skills on which you will be tested on the multiple-choice and direct-writing sections of the exam. On this list are skills within the categories of *sentence formation, usage,* and *mechanics.* We've gone over it with a fine-tooth comb so that by the time you finish Lesson 8, you'll have thoroughly reviewed every one.

Don't worry. That doesn't mean we're going to throw 196 rules of comma usage at you or tell you to memorize terms like "gerund" and "present perfect tense." It doesn't even mean that you need to be able to state grammatical rules and terms.

It *does* mean you need to know how to *apply* some of the key rules. When we explain these rules, it helps if you understand the key terms. It's like learning how to play basketball. You don't have to be able to talk like a sportscaster, but you do need to know what your coach means by a "foul" and a "free throw."

The only way to polish the old grammar skills is to start with the toolkit of grammar: *the parts of speech* (nouns, verbs, adjectives, and so on). Sound familiar? While we're filling your handy toolkit with grammar rules, we'll walk you through how to use them on multiple-choice questions just like those on the writing exam. Because practice items will be sprinkled throughout the grammar, usage, and mechanics review in this lesson and the next, let's call a time-out to review what these questions look like.

As we explained in Lesson 2, there are three types of multiple-choice questions.

1. **Planning Questions:** These are the questions that ask about a prewriting activity the pretend student does during the planning stage, before writing the rough draft.

2. **Composing and Revising Questions:** These are the questions that focus on the first section of the student's rough draft and how it might be improved.

3. **Editing Questions:** These are the ones that ask about the grammar and mechanics of a second section of the draft. You have to spot errors and recognize how they can be fixed.

We covered questions of the first two types in the last lesson, so let's move on to the third type—editing questions. Editing questions come in a couple of forms. Some ask you to edit for correct use of language (which people often refer to as "grammar and usage"), and others require you to edit for capitalization, punctuation, and spelling. In this lesson, we'll focus mainly on editing for correct use of language. Let's take a short time-out to go over what the directions look like.

THE DIRECTIONS

Now familiarize yourself with these directions, which are just like what you will see on the exam before that third type of multiple-choice question.

> **Read this next section of John's rough draft and answer questions 1–4. This section has groups of underlined words. The questions ask about these groups of underlined words.**

TIP: Remember: In about one out of four cases, "As it is" will be your answer.

According to these directions, your task is to read another section of the same draft you've read for the planning, composing, and revising questions. This time, each question gives you an underlined phrase from the draft. Sometimes the underlined phrase contains an error, and sometimes it doesn't. You have to figure out which of the four choices shows how that phrase would be written correctly.

Here's what one of these questions might look like.

▶ **In sentence 10, how would <u>if dogs does move their lips when they read</u> be correctly written?**

    A if dogs do move their lips when they read

    B if dogs does move its lips when they read

    C if dogs does move their lips when it reads

    D As it is

Okay, time-out's over. Back to the grammar review game.

NOUNS

A **noun** is the name of **a person, place,** or **thing** (which includes **ideas**). That's what every teacher from first grade on up has told you, right?

Person: Calvin, Sofia, wrestler, grandmother, president, sophomore

Place: Richmond, Potomac River, high school, street

Thing: popcorn, sweatshirt, credit card, Jeep Cherokee, history class

Idea: love, excellence, optimism, Boyle's Law

Nouns that name specific people, places, or things are capitalized. These are called *proper nouns*. Here are some examples: Bill Goldberg, Grandma, President Kennedy, Kingston High School, Blue Ridge Mountains, Tipperary Street, Korean War, World Championship Wrestling, *The History of the Western World.*

Note: Words like *president, high school,* and *war* may or may not be capitalized. It all depends on whether you are naming *a particular* president, high school, or war:

> Of all our *presidents, President* Kennedy was one of the most popular.

> I am a *high school* student at Alfred E. Neuman *High School.*

> The Civil *War* was one of the bloodiest *wars* of all time.

A noun may end in *-ing.* This is called a *gerund.* Here are some examples of gerunds: *giggling, munching, whistling, slurping.*

The subject of a sentence is a noun. What are the subjects of the two sentences below?

> Eating bamboo shoots is a panda's favorite activity.

> Watching 3-D TV shows is fun.

A noun may describe more than one person or thing. Then the noun is called *plural.* **Most plural nouns end in *-s*:** *sodas, dates, stadiums, jokes, videos.*

> Sodas are sugary.

> Videos are on sale.

> **TIP:** *Reminder* from Lesson 4: The subject of a sentence is the who or what that does the action. Check to make sure your sentence has a subject by making sure it answers the questions: "What is/does . . .?" or "Who is/does . . .?" What is a panda's favorite activity? Eating. What is fun? Watching.

REBEL NOUNS

Some nouns are rebels—they have *irregular* plural forms that you just have to memorize.

Some plural nouns end in *-es.* If a word ends in *-s, -x, -z, -ch,* or *-sh,* add *-es* to form the plural. The following chart should help demonstrate this phenomenon:

Singular	Plural
class	classes
boss	bosses
tax	taxes
fax	faxes
dish	dishes
watch	watches

Sometimes you need to double the final letter before ending *-es.*

bus busses (*buses* is fine too)

quiz quizzes (*quizes* is considered *wrong*)

Some plural nouns don't end in *-s* **(or** *-es***) at all.** For example: *men, women, children, geese, sheep, deer.*

Flying sheep are easy to count.

Deer are pretty but dumb.

Here are some more common rebels. Try covering up the right column and forming the irregular plurals on your own first.

Singular Noun	Irregular Plural noun
woman	women
mouse	mice
goose	geese
cdeer	deer
alumnus	alumni
datum	data

Some nouns end in *-s* **but are not plural.** Here are some examples: *mathematics, news, politics, statistics* (as in the branch of mathematics).

Mathematics is his worst subject.

Statistics is interesting to her.

Some nouns look plural but aren't. Here are some examples: *United States, family, committee.* They do stand for several individuals but are singular—and take singular verbs—because they describe *one single group.*

The United States is a fairly young country.

My family is nutty enough to be on a sitcom.

Phew! We've gone over a lot of noun rules—including some rules about how to spell plural nouns. (In the next lesson, we'll review a lot of the spelling rules the EOC exam-makers want you to know.) Let's take a moment to try out some multiple-choice questions based on our review so far. You may want to mark this page, since you will be using it to answer several other questions throughout the lesson.

Standardized Tests

Terry has decided to write a humorous letter to the editor of the school newspaper about standardized tests. Here is part of her rough draft. Use it to answer questions 1–3.

Dear Editor:

(1) Do you want to know what makes life worth living for <u>a High School junior</u> like me? (2) The answer is standardized tests. (3) Taking <u>test preparation clases is</u> more fun than buying scratch-off lottery tickets. (4) What could be more exciting than practicing <u>math and reading questions on Saturday</u> mornings with an SAT "coach"?

(5) My history and biology teachers may not win any <u>Academy Awards, but his review sessions</u> for the EOC Exam <u>make it entertaining.</u>

(6) In fact, <u>my classmates and me are</u> thinking of designing a special trophy. (7) <u>One wishes to show</u> appreciation to all those teachers who make testing so much fun. (8) Seriously, though, we should be grateful to teachers for their efforts to see that we pass these exams. (9) They have always been put a lot of pressure to see that their students do well, and in the future they will be held even more "accountable" for how their students do.

---

1   In sentence 1, how would <u>a High School junior</u> be correctly written?

   A   a High School Junior
   B   a high school Junior
   C   a high school junior
   D   As it is

2   In sentence 3, how would <u>test preparation clases</u> be correctly written?

   F   test preparation classes
   G   Test Preparation Clases
   H   test prepearation clases
   J   As it is

3   In sentence 4, how would <u>math and reading questions on Saturday</u> be correctly written?

   A   math and reading questions on saturday
   B   Math and Reading questions on Saturday
   C   math and reading questiones on Saturday
   D   As it is

Check the answer key on page 65 for the correct answers.

PRONOUNS

A pronoun is a word that takes the place of a noun. Think of them as stand-ins. We use a lot of pronouns in everyday English instead of repeating names and words over and over. Here are some examples: *I, you, he, she, it, we, they, who, anyone, something, somebody, me, him, her, us, them, whom, mine, yours, his, hers, ours, theirs, whose, myself, yourself, himself, itself, ourselves, themselves.*

The word a pronoun stands in for is called the *antecedent.*

   Cathy gave away *her* dessert.

In this sentence, *her* stands in for Cathy. So the antecedent is *Cathy*.

   My mother, *who* argued with the ref, felt pretty silly when he offered her his mask.

Who replaces *my mother*. The antecedent is *my mother*.

He replaces *the ref*. The antecedent is *the ref*.

I have e-mailed my cousin Daniel, who lives in Norfolk, to invite *him* to my graduation.

Him replaces *my cousin Daniel*. The antecedent is *my cousin Daniel*.

The pronoun must agree with its antecedent in gender and number. In other words, check whether a pronoun should be masculine or feminine, singular or plural, by looking back at the word it replaces. Make sure there's a match. Ask yourself, "Is the pronoun masculine (or feminine)?" "Is the pronoun singular (or plural)?"

I called my brother, Wesley, who has his license, to ask *him* for a ride home.

Singular? Check. *Him* matches *Wesley*. Masculine? Check.

When people offer you something for free, ask yourself what *they* want in return.

Plural? Check. *They* matches *people*. Both masculine and feminine? Check.

Now find the pronoun that agrees with the antecedent:

Goldberg played football on two NFL teams before ___ became a wrestler.

Easy, right? Goldberg played football on two NFL teams before *he* became a wrestler. Here's one that's a little harder:

The wrestling organization has cast him as a good guy, but ____ might change him into a villain.

Careful, here. Did you put *they* in the blank? Well, if so, you're wrong!

Correct version: The wrestling organization has cast him as a good guy, but *it* might change him into a villain.

The pronoun that goes in the blank is a stand-in for *the wrestling organization*. The pronoun must be *singular,* then, and neither masculine nor feminine. *The wrestling organization* is not a *he* or a *she*. The organization is not a plural *they*, either—because it stands for *one* single group, like "family" or "committee." The wrestling organization is a singular *it*. Note that there's also a clue early in the sentence that points to the fact that *organization* is singular: It's followed by a singular verb: "The wrestling organization *has* . . ."

PRONOUN REFERENCE
Make pronouns point clearly to what they replace. Sometimes you may know to what you're referring—but your reader might not.

Unclear. Don't take the lid off the ice cream if you're going to put it there.

Does *it* refer to the lid or the ice cream? We can't be sure.

Clear. Don't take the lid off the ice cream if you're going to put the ice cream there.

Unclear. Cal asked his father if he could play the banjo.

Does *he* refer to Cal or his father? The "he" is ambiguous.

Clear. Cal asked his father if his father could play the banjo.

PRONOUN CASE

Do you know what "pronoun case" is? No, it isn't what you carry your pronouns in. Case refers to a noun or pronoun's form. There are three, and Virginia students are expected to know when to use which one. Here's a chart that shows the three cases.

    Subjective case: *I, you, he/she, it, we, they, who, one, anybody*

    Objective case: *me, you, him/her, it, us, them, whom, one, anybody*

    Possessive case: *my, your, his/her, its, our, their, whose, one's, anybody's*

When the subject is a pronoun, you need to use the *subjective* case.

    Incorrect: Them are my batting gloves. Us are going to the practice field.

    Correct: They are my batting gloves. We are going to the practice field.

It's pretty easy to tell which pronoun is correct, right?

Compound Subjects

Me or I? Things get trickier when you have a compound subject (two or more subjects joined by *and*).

    Incorrect: Ali and me want to go to the game. Them and us are rivals.

This is one of the most common types of grammatical errors, because it is one that so many of us use incorrectly from the time we learn to talk.

    Correct: Ali and I want to go to the game. They and we are rivals.

Tip: To figure out whether you need *me* or *I*, try splitting up the sentence this way.

    Ali wants to go to the game.

    ___ want to go to the game.

What goes in the blank—*I* or *me*? Yes, you would say: *I* want to go to the game.

    Correct: *Ali* and *I* want to go to the game.

Try *them* and *us* by splitting it up the same way.

_____ are rivals. They are rivals.

_____ are rivals. We are rivals.

_____ and _____ are rivals.

Correct: *They* and *we* are rivals.

That may sound weird because it's not always how we tend to talk, but remember: You shouldn't base your answers to these questions on what *sounds* right. What sounds right in this case isn't.

Rule: The pronoun in a compound subject has to be the same as if it were standing alone. Let's correct a few more together.

Incorrect: Frank and me are brothers.

_____ is a brother.

_____ am a brother.

_____ and _____ are brothers.

Correct: *Frank* and *I* are brothers.

Incorrect: My mother and me are going to the mall.

_____ is going to the mall.

_____ am going to the mall.

_____ and _____ are going to the mall.

Correct: *My mother* and *I* are going to the mall.

Me As a Direct or Indirect Object

The object of a sentence is the person or thing affected by the verb. It can be direct or indirect.

He gave me all the red jellybeans.

The direct object is *jellybeans* and the indirect object is *me*. Why is this? Who or what does he give? *Jellybeans.* To whom or to what are they given? *Me.*

To figure out whether a word is a direct or indirect object, ask yourself: Is this the person or thing that is (verb)ed? If yes, it is a direct object.

Is this the person to or for whom the (verb)ing gets done? If yes, it is an indirect object.

Try this on the sentence below.

Tanya owes me five dollars.

The *five dollars* is the direct object. It describes *what* is owed. The word *me* is the indirect object. It tells the person *to whom* all this owing is getting done.

We talked before about being careful to use *I* in the subjective case—whether it's *I* alone or with someone else:

Correct: Tanya and I are friends. I am her friend.

A similar rule applies to the objective case. Be careful to use *me* —whether the *me* to whom or for whom something is happening stands alone or with someone else.

Incorrect: Our parents gave Luan and I a trip to Vietnam as a graduation present.

You have a *compound object* here—two people to whom a trip was given, joined by *and.*

To figure out what pronoun you should use in a compound object, try splitting up the sentence—as you did previously when checking agreement of compound subjects.

Our parents gave _____ a trip to Vietnam. Our parents gave *Luan* a trip to Vietnam.

Our parents gave _____ a trip to Vietnam. Our parents gave *me* a trip to Vietnam.

Correct: Our parents gave *Luan* and *me* a trip to Vietnam for graduation.

Try a couple more.

Please pass the mashed potatoes to Malcolm and ___. (*me*)

Angie and ___ are both trying out for the play. (*I*)

It's hard for Suki and _____ to get there without a car. (*me*)

Point of View

The point of view refers to who is telling a story—the "voice" behind a piece of writing.

Maintain a consistent point of view. Say you decide to write a sports report about a recent lacrosse match. If you played in the game, you might talk about *I* and *we*, but if you were in the bleachers, you would talk about *he* or *she* and *they*.

See if you can tell how the underlined words cause an improper shift in the point of view, below.

> Some toothbrush ads claim that regular brushing could add years to your life. Studies suggest that if one has gum disease, you are more likely to have heart disease. Taking care of your gums prevents tooth loss and it may help <u>one's</u> heart too.

How do you correct the problem? Since the speaker is talking to *you* throughout this piece, *one* and *one's* should be changed to *you* and *your*. Now you try a few of these questions based on Terry's draft about standardized tests (page 57).

4   In sentence 5, how would <u>Academy Awards, but his review sessions</u> be correctly written?

    F   Academy Awards, but their review sessions

    G   academy awards, but his review sessions

    H   Academy Awards, but his review sessiones

    J   As it is

5   In sentence 5, how would <u>make it entertaining</u> be correctly written?

    A   make them entertaining

    B   make the review entertaining

    C   make it wonderful entertainment

    D   As it is

6   In sentence 6, how would <u>my classmates and me are</u> be correctly written?

    F   Me and my classmates

    G   my classmates and me is

    H   my classmates and I are

    J   As it is

7 In sentence 7, how would <u>One wishes to show</u> be correctly written?

    A We wish to show

    B They wish to show

    C You wish to show

    D As it is

Check your answers on page 65.

PRONOUNS ARE COOL

Well, maybe not, but perhaps this little mnemonic will help you remember all this stuff. To check for correct pronoun use, ask yourself: Do these **P**ronouns **A**gree with their antecedents and are they in the proper **C**ase?

SUMMARY

Trim the Fat and Keep the Lean: Get rid of unnecessary words.

Process of Elimination (POE): Eliminate any choices that create new problems.

Pronouns Are Cool: Check the pronouns for agreement and case.

ANSWER KEY

1 C Proper nouns—capitalization. The proper name of a particular high school would go in caps. Do not capitalize general class names—freshman, sophomore, junior, or senior.

2 F Plural nouns—spelling. To form the plural of a word that ends in *-s*, add *-es*.

3 D Proper nouns—capitalization. Capitalize names of days of the week, not words that describe general subjects.

4 F Pronoun-antecedent agreement. Whenever there's a pronoun among the underlined words, check that the pronoun agrees with its antecedent. In this case, *his* doesn't agree with its antecedent. The word *their* should stand in place of *my history and biology teachers'*.

5 B Pronoun reference. It needs to be clear who or what a pronoun is replacing. What does *it* stand for—the EOC exam? No. The version in choice **B** clarifies that it is the review itself that is entertaining.

6 H Compound subject. In compound subject situations, use *I*, not *me*.

7 A Consistent point of view. Terry is speaking directly throughout this piece ("I" and "We"). There is no reason to switch mid-stream to a different point of view ("One," "They," or "You").

LESSON 5
EDITING QUESTIONS:
VERBS, ADJECTIVES, AND ADVERBS

VERBS
Next up in our review of grammar are verbs.

Some verbs express actions. Here are some examples: *snore, waken, wash, brush, gobble, rush, burp, sit, dream, chat, munch, remember, wink, smooch.*

Some verbs describe states of being. Here are some examples: *am, seem, appear, become, remain.*

There are all sorts of verb topics we might cover, but for the EOC English: Writing Exam, three are particularly important: *Tense, Irregular Forms*, and *Voice*. Some EOC exam questions require you to recognize when the wrong tense is being used, and others require you to spot the wrong form. Still others test that you know how to keep the "voice" (active or passive) consistent. Sometimes two or three of these errors are rolled into one.

TENSE
What does "tense" mean here? No, it doesn't have anything to do with stressed and uptight. Tense refers to *when* the verb's action takes place.

Today I snore.	Present Tense
Yesterday I snored.	Past Tense
I have always snored.	Present Perfect Tense
I will snore.	Future Tense
I will have snored.	Future Perfect Tense

To form the past tense, add *-ed*. Most verbs follow this nice, simple rule: *snore + -ed = snored.*

IRREGULAR VERB FORMS

Unfortunately, a bunch of common verbs don't follow this nice rule, and these (of course!) are the verbs on which the EOC Exam might test you. There's a good reason for this. Like it or not, you will find that people such as college admissions officers and job interviewers mark you down when you use the wrong verb form in speaking or writing.

TIP: It's a good idea to read most of this lesson aloud, especially sentences that demonstrate the correct ways of saying things. There is a difference between written English and spoken English because the rules of spoken grammar are much looser. Written English is much more rigid, and you are probably not as used to hearing it aloud.

The following chart will review some of the verbs that don't follow the rules. As long as you learn the "irregular" verbs on the chart and remember the rules for all the other "regular" verbs, you'll be ready to spot any verb form error the EOC Exam tosses at you. It's a good idea to read the chart across, out loud. Then try quizzing yourself by using a sheet of paper to cover up the past and future forms as you say them.

Present Today I . . .	Past Yesterday I . . .	Present Perfect I have always/never . . .	Future I will . . .	Future Perfect I will have. . .
Begin	began	begun	begin	begun
bite	bit	bitten	bite	bitten
break	broke	broken	break	broken
build	built	built	build	built
buy	bought	bought	buy	bought
catch	caught	caught	catch	caught
choose	chose	chosen	choose	chosen
come	came	come	come	come
do	did	done	do	done
draw	drew	drawn	draw	drawn
drink	drank	drunk	drink	drunk
drive	drove	driven	drive	driven
eat	ate	eaten	eat	eaten
fall	fell	fallen	fall	fallen
feed	fed	fed	feed	fed
feel	felt	felt	feel	felt
fight	fought	fought	fight	fought
find	found	found	find	found
fly	flew	flown	fly	flown
forget	forgot	forgotten	forget	forgotten
forgive	forgave	forgiven	forgive	forgiven
freeze	froze	frozen	freeze	frozen
get	got	gotten	get	gotten
give	gave	given	give	given
go	went	gone	go	gone
grow	grew	grown	grow	grown
have	had	had	have	had

hold	held	held	hold	held
hurt	hurt	hurt	hurt	hurt
know	knew	known	know	known
lead	led	led	lead	led
leave	left	left	leave	left
lend	lent	lent	lend	lent
let	let	let	let	let
lie	lay	lain	lie	lain
lay	laid	laid	lay	laid
lose	lost	lost	lose	lost
make	made	made	make	made
meet	met	met	meet	met
put	put	put	put	put
read	read	read	read	read
ride	rode	ridden	ride	ridden
rise	rose	risen	rise	risen
run	ran	run	run	run
see	saw	seen	see	seen
sell	sold	sold	sell	sold
send	sent	sent	send	sent
set	set	set	set	set
shine	shone	shone	shine	shone
shrink	shrank	shrunk	shrink	shrunk
sing	sang	sung	sing	sung
sink	sank	sunk	sink	sunk
sit	sat	sat	sit	sat
sleep	slept	slept	sleep	slept
speak	spoke	spoken	speak	spoken
steal	stole	stolen	steal	stolen
stick	stuck	stuck	stick	stuck
strike	struck	struck	strike	struck
sweep	swept	swept	sweep	swept
wim	swam	swum	swim	swum
swing	swung	swung	swing	swung
take	took	taken	take	taken
teach	taught	taught	teach	taught
tear	tore	torn	tear	torn
tell	told	told	tell	told
think	thought	thought	think	thought
throw	threw	thrown	throw	thrown
wear	wore	worn	wear	worn
win	won	won	win	won
write	wrote	written	write	written

Whoa! That's a lot to digest all at once. Let's take small bites at first.

TENSE

How do you know when to use what? Well, luckily, most sentences contain clues to tense. Even verbs like the irregular ones above follow certain rules. Remember this: **Maintain tense consistency.** Don't shift tenses mid-sentence or mid-paragraph unless you really mean to indicate a shift in time. In other words, don't write the way so many people talk: ". . . And then I said . . . and she says . . . and finally he said . . ."

Look at this sentence.

> Because parents complained about starting times, the Board of Education _____ to change the schedule.

What form of *decide* goes in the blank? The answer is *decided*. The sentence began in the past tense, so it is simplest to keep the rest of the sentence in the past tense, too. The complaints and the decision were both in the past, right?

Certain words will clue you in to the fact that you need the future tense: *tomorrow, later, in the future, next (time/week/year), some (-day,-time).*

> Tomorrow I _____ my book. Tomorrow *I will read* my book.

Others signal that the past tense is needed: *yesterday, in the past, before that, at first, then, years ago, recently, last (Monday/month/summer/time/year).*

> Yesterday I _____ my book. Yesterday *I read* my book.

Still others signal that special past tenses are required: *since, until, before, after, while, for (days/weeks/years).*

> Every St. Patrick's Day since 1998, Erin _____ her hair green.

> Every St. Patrick's Day since 1998, Erin *has tinted* her hair green.

> Before becoming governor, he _____ as mayor.

> Before becoming governor, he *had served* as mayor.

> While the principal *was deciding*, students *held* their breath.

> After teachers *had spoken* in favor of the change, students *shared* their experiences.

Some "time" words signal that one action will be completed in the future before another future action: *until, when, as soon as*.

We will not give it away *until* we have spoken with you.

As soon as we have decided, we will let you know.

Finally, the tense of other verbs in a sentence often determines what tense you need.

When your teacher *mentions* Leonardo Da Vinci, she *is not talking* about the actor in *Titanic*.

Both actions are happening in the present.

The football player *was running* toward the end-zone when he *tripped*.

Here, one action was going on when another one happened.

When Jeremy finally *called* Sara he *sounded* nervous.

Both actions happened in the past.

Verb tense should remain consistent. If most of a paragraph takes place in the future, chances are that any verbs you are asked to fill in should be in the future as well.

There will be many changes in the next 1,000 years. We will drive cars that fly and we will probably travel freely to outer space. Maybe we _____ time travel. I hope we will be able to save the whales and control the weather.

The whole paragraph is full of predictions about the future, right? So what goes in the blank? What makes sense and is consistent with the tense throughout the paragraph?

Maybe we *will have* time travel.

If the paragraph is in the past tense, chances are that any missing verbs should also be in the past tense.

In his last comic strip, Charles Schulz thanked his readers. He _____ them he considered himself fortunate to draw Charlie Brown and his pals for nearly 50 years. He said that he could never forget Charlie Brown, Snoopy, Lucy and all the others.

Did you put *told* in the blank? That's right, since the other verbs are in the past tense.

VOICE

Do you know what "voice" means here? No, it's not about singing, but it does have to do with how you say something. Often you can say the same thing in two ways.

TIP: *Remember:* Make sure verb tense is consistent with word clues in the sentence, as well as with the meaning of the passage.

Active voice. He did his math homework. He is taking a break.

Passive voice. His math homework was done by him. A break is being taken by him.

There are two rules about voice to keep in mind.

1. **Be consistent.** If most of a piece of writing is in the active voice, keep it that way. Don't suddenly switch to passive.

2. **KISS = Keep it short and simple.** In the examples above, which is shorter and simpler—the statements in active or passive voice? Yup, the ones in the active voice. The clearest and most direct way of saying something is often in the active voice.

Now that you have verb forms under your belt, let's talk about subject-verb agreement.

Remember how we said that pronouns have to be agreeable? They have to agree with their antecedents? Well, verbs have to be agreeable, too—only they have to answer to their subjects!

SUBJECT-VERB AGREEMENT

The verb must agree with the subject in number. In other words, if the subject is singular, the verb is singular.

> The bullfrog croaks.

If the subject is plural, the verb is plural.

> The bullfrogs croak.

You may be asking how you can tell whether the subject is singular or plural in the first place. If you aren't sure whether the subject in a sentence is singular or plural, try the "He/She/It/They" Test.

- If you can replace the subject of a sentence with *he, she*, or *it*, the subject is singular.

- If you can replace the naming part of a sentence with *they*, the subject is probably plural.

He/She:

The student takes five classes a day.

The subject, *student*, is singular and requires a singular verb, *takes*.

They:

Some students go off-campus for lunch.

The subject, *some students*, is plural and requires a plural verb, *go*.

Easy, huh? Things do get a bit more complicated when there are words between the subject and verb.

The bullfrog *sitting in a cluster of lily pads* croaks.

The bullfrogs *sitting on the log* croak.

To make sure subject and verb agree, just follow **Thelma's Rule of Thumb.**

First, find the subject: the *who, what,* or *that* the sentence is mainly about.

The bullfrog sitting in a cluster of lily pads croaks.

Now, put the tip of your thumb down right after the subject *(bullfrog)*. Cover all the extra words that come between the subject and the verb *(sitting in a cluster of lily pads)*.

Then, make sure the verb agrees with the subject in number. (Since *bullfrog* is a singular subject, it takes a singular verb—*croaks*).

VERBS ARE TICKLISH

Sound weird? Don't worry; this is just another mnemonic to help you remember to watch out for Agreement and Tense. You don't have to say it out loud in front of people. Just remember the first letter of every word:

Verbs:

Are: Agreement

Ticklish: Tense

> **TIP:** Remember: Think of all those words between the subject and verb as gobbledy-gook. Ignore them. The word *pads* is a plural noun, but don't let that fool you into choosing a plural verb for the word next door. *Pads* is not the subject, bullfrog is. *Pads* is just extra stuff under your thumb.

So now, if one of the underlined phrases contains a verb, you can use this memory aid to eliminate choices that are wrong. Plug each choice into the sentence and ask yourself:

Is the **V**erb in **A**greement with its subject?

Is this the proper **T**ense?

Only one choice should meet both requirements and that's your answer. Now is a good time to stop and put what we've reviewed into action.

Carter's health teacher has asked her class to write essays on how students handle stress. Carter has decided to write about students in all four grades at his high school.

Read this section of Carter's rough draft and answer questions 1–9. This section has groups of underlined words. The questions ask about these groups of underlined words.

(1) Having too much to do and too little time <u>became a problem for everyone</u> at Ogden Ogilvie sooner or later. (2) Ninth grade is a difficult time. (3) <u>Many ninth graders are</u> shell-shocked by the change from middle school to high school. (4) Gone are those carefree middle-school days. (5) With more homework, <u>there are less hours</u> in the day for free time. (6) Stress <u>can be even worser</u> in tenth grade. (7) <u>Sudden increases in homework is</u> accompanied by a decrease in sleep. (8) Many juniors long for the weekend, when <u>they can lay in bed</u> as long as they want. (9) My fellow juniors agree, though, that <u>stress is felt by them the most</u> in the 11th grade. (10) This is the big year, the one that counts. (11) <u>Many juniors who are bound for college</u> feel lucky if they can still stand up <u>by June after prepared</u> for the EOC exams, PSATs, SATs, and, in some cases, AP exams. (12) The stress is felt by all grades at Ogden Ogilvie, but students at all levels <u>have always finded</u> ways to handle it.

(13) <u>Freshmen take time to relax</u> by lounging in the cafeteria. (14) <u>Many go regular</u> to the Regal to see a new release and play video games. (15) Since few have licenses, freshmen also learn that <u>one of the wonderfullest stress-busters</u> is walking. (16) Some of <u>the most popular escapes include</u> hanging out at the mall, working out at the gym, and getting rides from upperclassmen. (17) To get away from the alphabet soup of tests, many juniors, on the other hand, <u>head quick</u> for the road. (18) My friends and I like to get in the car and just drive until we run out of gas, although <u>I don't see no way</u> for that particular form of relaxation to continue if the price of gas keeps rising.

1   In sentence 1, how would <u>became a problem for everyone</u> be correctly
    written?

    A had become a problem for everyone
    B becomes a problem for everyone
    C become a problem for everyone
    D As it is

2   In sentence 3, how would <u>Many ninth graders are</u> be correctly written?

    F Many ninth graders is
    G Many ninth graders was
    H Many ninth graders will be
    J As it is

3   In sentence 7, how would <u>Sudden increases in homework is</u> be correctly
    written?

    A Sudden increases in homework were
    B Sudden increases in homework being
    C Sudden increases in homework are
    D As it is

4   In sentence 8, how would <u>they can lay in bed</u> be correctly written?

    F they can lie in bed
    G you can lay in bed
    H one can lay in bed
    J As it is

5   In sentence 9, how would <u>stress is felt by them the most</u> be correctly
    written?

    A stress were felt by them the most
    B they feel the most stress
    C stress is felt by them the mostest
    D As it is

6 In sentence 11, how would <u>who are bound for college feel</u> be correctly written?

    F whom are bound for college feel

    G who is bound for college feel

    H who are bound for college feels

    J As it is

7 In sentence 11, how would <u>by June after prepared</u> be correctly written?

    A by june after preparing

    B by June after having preparing

    C by June after preparing

    D As it is

8 In sentence 12, how would <u>have always finded</u> be correctly written?

    F have always found

    G always finds

    H has always finded

    J As it is

9 In sentence 13, how would <u>Freshmen take time to relax</u> be correctly written?

    A Freshmen takes time to relax

    B Freshmen taken time to relax

    C Time is taken by freshmen to relax

    D As it is

Check your answers on page 83.

Voila! Nouns and verbs are all covered. All that's left in this grammar review are adjectives and adverbs.

ADJECTIVES AND ADVERBS

On the exam, you may have to identify errors in which adjectives and adverbs are mistakenly switched. You'll need to know when to use one or the other. We'll review them together.

Adjectives **describe nouns.** They often describe a person or thing's appearance, sound, taste, smell, or feel: *flashing* lights, *loud* music, *salty* peanuts, *sweaty* odor, *sticky* floor.

Adverbs **usually describe verbs—but sometimes, describe adjectives.** They often describe how, when, or where the action takes place: arrive *late*, dance *wildly*, slip *suddenly*, laugh *loudly*, leave *early*.

Adverbs often—but not always—end in *-ly*.

ADJECTIVES VERSUS ADVERBS

Adjective	Adverb
You are a bad dog.	You are drooling badly. (*not* You are drooling bad.)
She is a happy camper.	She whistles happily. (*not* She whistles happy.)
There is slow traffic ahead.	You should drive slowly. (*not* You should drive slow.)
My snail is slower than yours.	He moves more slowly than yours. (*not* He moves more slow than yours.)
The departures are frequent.	The planes depart frequently. (*not* They depart more frequent.)
She is a good player.	She played well. (*not* She played good.)
his is a real autograph.	It is really authentic. (*not* It is real authentic.)

COMPARISONS

Be careful how you use adjectives and adverbs to make comparisons. Use the following chart to help you use your adverbs and adjectives correctly.

one person or thing	two people or things	three or more people or things
The soup is hot.	This soup is hotter than that one.	This soup is hottest of all.
My foot is tiny.	My foot is tinier than yours.	My foot is the tiniest of all.
Pumpkins are scarce.	Mice are scarcer.	Coachmen are scarcest of all.
The food is great.	The entertainment is greater.	The dancing is greatest of all.
I am beautiful.	I am more beautiful than you.	I am the most beautiful of all.

Most adjectives, like *hot* **and** *tiny*, **follow a nice rule: Add** *-er* **or** *-est*. But, of course, there always has to be an exception to the rule, doesn't there? For example, with a longer adjective, such as *beautiful*, you couldn't just add an *-er*.

TIP: Here's a little rhyme to help you remember comparative forms of adjectives:
When the word is e-nor-**mous**
With word endings do not **fuss**
If three syllables or **more**
Put "more" or "most" **before**
Well, I tried!

Incorrect. I am not *beautifuller* than you.

Correct. I am *more beautiful* than you.

Adjective	Comparative	Superlative
huge	huger	hugest
enormous	more enormous	most enormous
zany	zanier	zaniest
idiotic	more idiotic	most idiotic
smart	smarter	smartest
intelligent	more intelligent	most intelligent

Now you've got adjectives down pat. On to adverbs.

There are a few adverbs that take only an *-er* or *-est* ending to show comparison. Since there are only a few, learn the common ones now.

soon	sooner	soonest
early	earlier	earliest
well	better	best

Most adverbs take *more* or *most* instead of *-er* or *-est* endings.

drowsily	more drowsily	most drowsily
rapidly	more rapidly	most rapidly
warmly	more warmly	most warmly

My baby is the prettiest.

You don't say, "My baby is the *most* prettiest." *Prettiest* already means most. "Most" is already built in so you don't have to say it again. You can't get any prettier than the prettiest.

TIP: When it comes to comparative forms of adjectives and adverbs, trim the fat.
Don't stick in extra words, such as **more** and **most,** when they are unnecessary.

SOL PET PEEVES

We've all had English teachers with pet peeves. Maybe you had Ms. Syntax, who was a stickler for irregular verbs and had a particular thing with the word *shrink*. Remember how horrified she was by the film title, *Honey, I Shrunk the Kids*? If the guys in Hollywood had consulted with Ms. Syntax, they would've called the comedy classic, *Honey I Shrank the Kids*. Well, the people responsible for the SOL have certain pet peeves, too. There are certain errors you hear all the time in spoken English—and they want to make sure you keep them out of your writing.

Lay and Lie

There are two words on the list that are especially important to know. The EOC exam-makers have singled out one particular error they especially want you to avoid: the confusion of *lay* and *lie*. A big reason for the common mix-up is that the present tense of one is just like the past tense of the other.

Correct: Today I lie on the beach.   Today I lay my blanket on the beach.

Correct: Yesterday I lay on the beach.   Yesterday I laid my blanket on the beach.

Maybe it will help to read these little stories aloud a few times.

Yesterday I was so tired. I wanted so badly to *lie* down. "Now I *lie* down!" I finally cried. I *lay* down on my bed for a while. I *lay* there the whole afternoon. My mother yelled upstairs and I decided I *had lain* there long enough. I *have never lain* in bed so long. Tomorrow I *will lie* there for as long as I like. I *will have lain* there for the whole day when my mother comes home from her shift.

I lost my keys. I *lay* them down in a different place every day. Yesterday I *laid* them on the counter. The day before I *laid* them on the microwave. I have *always laid* them somewhere new. I *will lay* them in a special place if I find them. I *will have laid* them in that place every single day for a year before I ever lose them again.

DOUBLE NEGATIVES

Another pet peeve is double negatives. Appreciate the educators who made up the writing exam for wanting to help you save your breath and say what you mean. Double negatives waste words and they reverse what you really intend to say:

> **Double Negative:** I'm *not* paying *nothing* for that piece of junk!

> **Means:** I'm paying something for that piece of junk!

That's not what you really mean to say, is it?

Just as many adjectives already mean *more* or *most*, many words have *not* built in.

If you're already using *not* or the contraction *-n't* in the sentence, don't use the words *no, none, nothing, never, no one,* and *nobody*.

> **Incorrect:** I didn't see no way out. He can't have none of this. She could not find nothing.

> **Correct:** I didn't see any way out. He can't have any of this. She could not find anything.

Another way to fix these is to use the negative word and take out *not*.

> **I saw *no* way out. He can have *none* of this. She could find *nothing*.**

It doesn't matter which way you correct the error. Just choose *one* negative word and go with it.

LESS/FEWER

A third pet peeve of the SOL testers is confusion over *less* and *fewer*. Let's clear up that confusion forever.

> I have less money than you.

> I have less trouble than you.

> I have fewer dollars than you.

> I have fewer problems than you.

The rule is: If you can count 'em 1-2-3, use *fewer*. You can count dollars and problems. However, if you're not talking about separate things you can count, use *less*. "Money" does not refer to separate items—nor does "trouble"—so use *less*.

It's time once again to practice what we preach. See if you can apply what we've reviewed to some more questions based on Carter's draft (page 74).

10 In sentence 5, how would <u>there are less hours</u> be correctly written?

　　F　there are fewer hours

　　G　there is fewer hours

　　H　there is less hours

　　J　As it is

11 In sentence 6, how would <u>can be even worser</u> be correctly written?

　　A　can be even badder

　　B　can be even more worser

　　C　can be even worse

　　D　As it is

12 In sentence 14, how would <u>Many go regular</u> be correctly written?

　　F　Many goes regular

　　G　Many go regularly

　　H　Many went regular

　　J　As it is

13 In sentence 15, how would <u>one of the wonderfullest stress-busters</u> be correctly written?

　　A　one of the most wonderful stress-busters is

　　B　one of the wonderfullest stress-busters are

　　C　one of the most wonderful stress-busters are

　　D　As it is

14 In sentence 16, how would <u>the most popular escapes include</u> be correctly written?

    F the more popular escapes includes

    G the most popular escapes includes

    H the popularest escapes include

    J As it is

15 In sentence 17, how would <u>head quick</u> be correctly written?

    A heads quick

    B headed quick

    C head quickly

    D As it is

16 In sentence 18, how would <u>I don't see no way</u> be correctly written?

    F I don't see any way

    G I do not see no way

    H I haven't seen no way

    J As it is

Check the answer key on page 84 for the correct answers.

SUMMARY

Thelma's Rule of Thumb: To check for subject-verb agreement, squash everything in between the subject and the action it is performing.

Verbs Are Ticklish: Check verbs for agreement and tense.

KISS: Keep it short and simple when you have a choice of wording.

ANSWER KEY

1   **B**   **Verb tense.** The phrase *sooner or later* signals that the present tense, used consistently throughout the essay, is needed here, as well.

2   **J**   **Subject-verb agreement.** Many *are*. A plural subject (many) takes a plural verb.

3   **C**   **Subject-verb agreement.** Use Thelma's Rule of Thumb (see page 73) to avoid being distracted by the words between the plural subject (increases) and the plural verb it requires (are).

4   **F**   **Common usage problems—Lie/Lay.** They can *lie* in bed (but they can *lay* a blanket on the bed!).

5   **B**   **Active/passive voice.** Remember: KISS. The active voice is used throughout this essay. Why switch to a passive voice and create a longer, more complicated version when you don't need to? By POE, you can get rid of A (singular subject, *stress*, doesn't agree with plural verb, *were*) and **C** (*mostest* is an incorrect adjective comparison) even if you don't recognize the active/passive problem in the original.

6   **J**   **Pronoun case and subject-verb agreement.** Use Thelma's Rule of Thumb (page 73): *juniors* (plural) *feel* (plural). Only use "whom" when you need objective case—*to whom* or *for whom* or *with whom* or *from whom*.

7   **C**   **Verb tense.** Looking at the choices alone, you can discard every one but **C** by POE because of the errors you find. The month "June" isn't capitalized in **A**. Choices **B** and **D** are wrong because the time word *after* should be followed by either "preparing" or "having prepared."

8   **F**   **Verbs—common irregular forms.** If you know your verbs, *finded* doesn't look right. Before you look at the answers, you can guess aggressively that "have always found" is the answer—and there it is in **F**.

9   **D**   **Subject-verb agreement: active voice.** Remember—one out of four of these will be right, so if it looks right, it may well be right! Check that your **V**erbs **A**re **T**icklish, and when you see that agreement and tense are fine, go with "As it is."

10 F Common usage problems—less/fewer. Hours can be counted (try it: 1, 2, 3 . . . 24), so you say *fewer hours*, not *less hours*.

11 C Adjective comparisons. Remember: bad, worse, worst. Backsolving works here. Without looking back at Terry's essay, you can eliminate **A** (because there's no "badder"), **B** (no "worser"), and **D** (no "even worser").

12 G Adverb/adjective confusion. *Regular* is an adjective. You are describing how often an action (go) takes place, so you need an adverb (*-ly* word that describes the verb) here.

13 A Adverb comparisons. Remember: When you have long adjectives or adverbs, use *most* before: most wonderful, most beautiful, most unhappily. Save *-est* for words that are short and sweet (like shortest and sweetest!).

14 J Subject-verb agreement. You can guess aggressively that the underlined section sounds fine as is, but check that the **V**erbs **A**re **T**icklish just to be sure. You find that the plural verb (*include*) matches its plural subject (*escapes*) and that present tense fits consistently with what's been going on throughout the piece, so your guess is confirmed.

15 C Adverb errors. Remember: In speaking, many people mistakenly switch adverbs and adjectives, so don't rely too much on your "ear" for these. The word *head* is a verb (action) and requires an adverb (*-ly* word) to describe it.

16 F Double negative error. Don't repeat yourself. The idea "no" is built into "don't," so there is no need for another "no" before "way." Correct such a double negative by saying either, *I don't see any way* or *I see no way.*

LESSON 6
MECHANICS: SPELLING AND CAPITALIZATION

Now that we've reviewed Grammar and Usage, it's time for Mechanics—the *M* in GUM.

The SOL requires you to recognize three types of "mechanics" errors.

- Spelling

- Capitalization

- Punctuation

SPELLING

Many commonly misspelled words are *homophones*—words that sound the same, but are spelled differently. Don't let these fool you on the EOC exam. Unfortunately, the only way to catch them is to memorize when you use each one, since you can't rely on spelling rules to tell them apart. Even your computer's spellchecker can't help you, since it just points out non-words—not homophones used in the wrong places.

FREQUENTLY MISUSED WORDS

for/four	I have *four* doggy treats *for* you, Fido.
your/you're	Find *your* hat or *you're* going to have cold ears.
its/it's	When the wild pony turned *its* head, I thought that *it's* unusual to see one wearing sunglasses.
their/they're /there	*They're* over *there* in *their* tent.
to/two/too	I am *too* hot, so I'm going *to* go swimming for *two* hours.
here/hear	Stand right *here* and you can *hear* someone whisper from way over there.
accept/except	I will *accept* late papers *except* when they are overdue.
affect/effect	I don't know how this will *affect* you, but it has had a big *effect* on me.
principal/principle	The high school *principal* believes in the *principle* that if something can go wrong, it will.
stationary/stationery	Put this paperweight on the *stationery* to keep it *stationary* when a breeze comes along.
who's/whose	*Who's* the one *whose* smelly socks fell out of his gym bag?
presents/presence	You can get me *presents* if you want, but your *presence* at my party is more than enough.
than/then	I was taller *than* my brother, *then* he got older and became taller *than* me.
threw/through	Mimi *threw* her computer *through* the window.
whether/weather	I don't know *whether* the *weather* is going to be good or not.

Sometimes it's not whole words—just similar-sounding endings—that get people confused.

-al and -le endings:	natur*al*, referr*al*, miner*al*	*but* pick*le*, hand*le*, and doub*le*
-ance, -ence, -ense endings:	dist*ance*, inst*ance*,	*but* differ*ence*, rever*ence*,resist*ance* def*ense*, non*sense*
-or and -er endings:	refrigerat*or*, fact*or*, predat*or*, direct*or*	*but* work*er*, butt*er*, litt*er*, ev*er*

A FEW BASIC RULES

There are a few basic spelling rules we need to review. Many of the misspellings you'll find on the EOC exam are mistakes in changing from one word form to another, such as present to past tense.

Get rid of the silent *e*. Drop the silent *e* before adding *-ing* or *-ed*.

use	using	used
paste	pasting	pasted
examine	examining	examined
excite	exciting	excited

Add *-ed* to verbs that end "vowel + consonant."

a, e, i, o, u are vowels. All other letters are consonants. Double the final consonant before adding *-ed* or *-ing*.

clap	clapped
kid	kidded
plop	plopped
cup	cupped
refer	referred
win	winning
tap	tapped

Warning: You emphasize or stress the second part of *refer*. You say re-*FER*. Therefore you double the *r*. R-E-F-E-R-R-E-D.

If the end of a word is *not stressed*, forget the doubling.

offer	offered
layer	layered
lather	lathered
mention	mentioned

Add the correct endings to words that end in *-y*. For words that end "consonant + y,"change the *y* to *i* before adding *-es, -er, -ed,* or *-ly*.

family	families
responsibility	responsibilities
ceremony	ceremonies
early	earlier
party	parties

. . . but *not* if the word ends "vowel + *y*."

monkey	monkeys
chimney	chimneys
pulley	pulleys

Use -*ly* to turn adjectives into adverbs (usually). To form an adverb, you usually just add -*ly* (even when there's already an *l* at the end).

slow	slowly
complete	completely
careful	carefully
final	finally

Exception: If there's an unaccented -*y* at the end, as with that trio of cheerful words—*happy, merry, gay*—change the *y* to *i* before adding -*ly*.

happy	happily
merry	merrily
gay	gaily

I **before** *E* **except after** *C*. When trying to choose between *ie* or *ei*, remember the old rhyme.

"Use *i* before *e*

Except after *c*,

Or, when the sound comes out *AY*

as in *neighbor* and *weigh*"

Note how these words follow the poem-rule: f*ie*ld, y*ie*ld, bel*ie*ve, n*ie*ce, p*ie*ce, but rec*ei*ve, dec*ei*ve, rec*ei*pt, **and** n*ei*ghbor, w*ei*gh, *ei*ght, r*ei*gn.

Unfortunately, there are two common words that this rhyme *won't* help you with: These exceptions to the rule are: *either* and *neither*.

SPELLING DEMONS

Here are some other frequently used words that you need to be able to spell correctly, and many break the usual spelling rules we've just gone over. Of course, they're just the sorts of commonly misspelled words you are likely to find on the writing exam.

Try different ways of making the ones you have trouble with "stick." Copy each one three times as you say it aloud. Practice dividing the words into syllables.

COMMONLY MISSPELLED WORDS

again	believe	country	enough
always	busy	does	every
among	color	done	for
answer	coming	early	awful
cough	easy	forty	forward
friend	guess	half	having
just	making	many	meant
minute	none	often	once
ready	receive	said	says
seems	separate	since	success
sure	surprise	tear	though
through	tired	tonight	trouble
truly	used	writing	wrong

Here are some words that are *never* right, but that may look correct because you see them used so often. Don't let the EOC exam-makers slip one over on you!

Alright: Never, never use this. It is not *all right* to use this because it is not a word.

Alot: You will hear this in *a lot* of conversation, but never join the words as one this way.

WORD BREAKS

What happens if you're writing along and you come to the end of a line? If you're using a word processor, the computer usually takes care of things by bumping any word that won't fit onto the next line.

When you're writing things out by hand, though, the EOC exam-scorers want you to know how to divide words correctly between syllables with a hyphen (-) at the end of the line. You can usually figure out where a syllable ends just by saying the word to yourself.

ac-com-plish   na-tion   gui-tar   lep-re-chaun   Mis-sis-sip-pi

Do you feel as if you're drowning in alphabet soup? Do you need to come up for air? Don't worry; you don't need to be able to cite all these spelling rules. On the EOC English: Writing exam, you just need to *apply* them. For practice, here's another piece of Carter's draft of the essay on coping with stress.

TIP: When you're writing your composition for the direct-writing component of the exam, remember that you can always use the dictionary if you forget where to put the hyphen.

Read this next section of Carter's rough draft and answer questions 1–4. This section has groups of underlined words. The questions ask about these groups of underlined words.

(18) With rising gas prices, <u>students, who like to hit the road, may</u> have to settle for a short cruise <u>to some favorite eaterys</u> along the Pike: Doughie Donuts, <u>Grampa Gino's, Biddy's bagels,</u> Bugsy's Burgers, and last but not least—<u>Dr Doolittle's Veggie Treats.</u> (19) Even the short drive helps relax these students, and the calories provide extra fuel to get them <u>happyly through another</u> grueling day.

(20) <u>For many seniors who's</u> minds are on college, anxiety builds until April, when they find out <u>whether they have been accepted</u> to college. (21) To reduce the negative <u>effects of all this pressure,</u> many twelfth graders let off steam through participation in sports and clubs. (22) Members of the senior class take part in <u>a lot of group activities</u> such as <u>the class barbecue Winter Carnival,</u> Earth Day Celebration, <u>International Night, and the prom.</u> (23) They spend some <u>Saturdays and Sundays visiting Colleges,</u> but they devote most weekends to parties with other seniors.

(24) After <u>four years of coping with stress, many</u> seniors seem to agree on one thing. (25) High school should be <u>a time of enjoyment, and freedom.</u> (26) <u>For many at Ogilvie each</u> year has brought a different kind of stress in the past. (27) The future will undoubtedly <u>hold new pressure's</u> too. (28) We can plan how to meet some of those <u>pressures however, we can't</u> anticipate all of them.

(29) <u>Iv'e come to realize that we really have nothing except</u> the present moment, anyway.

(30) I, for one, intend to cut back on my worrying and enjoy that present moment to the fullest. (31) <u>Wasn't it the poet Robert Herrick</u> who <u>said "Gather ye rosebuds while ye may"?</u>

1 In sentence 18, how would <u>to some favorite eaterys</u> be correctly written?

   A too some favorite eaterys

   B to some favrote eaterys

   C to some favorite eateries

   D As it is

2 In sentence 19, how would <u>happyly through another</u> be correctly written?

   F happily through another

   G happilly through another

   H happyly threw another

   J As it is

3 In sentence 20, how would <u>For many seniors who's</u> be correctly written?

   A For many seniors whose

   B Four many seniors who's

   C For many Seniors who's

   D As it is

4 In sentence 20, how would <u>whether they have been accepted</u> be correctly written?

   F weather they have been accepted

   G whether they has been accepted

   H whether they have been excepted

   J As it is

Check the answer key on page 93 for the correct answers.

CAPITALIZATION

To keep on the lookout for capitalization errors on EOC English: Writing exam passages, you need to remember three main rules:

Capitalize proper nouns. Names of *specific* people, places, and things: Grandma Jessie, Washington High School, Erin Bryant, February, General Equivalency Diploma, Rosetta Stone, Smithsonian Institution, Japanese, Antarctica, Hudson Avenue, Mississippi River. **But:** a grandmother, a high school, a junior, winter, a diploma.

Capitalize proper adjectives. You should capitalize describing words that refer to *specific* people, places, and things: *Spanish* language, *Catholic* religion, *French* pastry.

> **TIP: The "Any Old" Test:** Have you ever heard someone say "any old" when they mean "any *one*," meaning not any *particular* one? Give me any old pen. I don't care which one. That's not just any old shoe. It's a Superfly 400. Test whether a word is a specific name by seeing if you can put "any old" in front of it. If you can, it's not, and the word shouldn't be capitalized.

Warning: Be careful *not* to use a capital for the words these adjectives *describe* unless the words, themselves, are proper nouns! For example,

Swiss Alps but Swiss chocolate

Italian Riviera but Italian sausage

Latin America but Mexican dinner

Math I (specific course) but math class

the South (specific region) but travel south

Capitalize titles. Capitalize titles of books, songs, movies, TV shows, etc. For example,

A Raisin in the Sun

"Row, Row, Row Your Boat"

American Beauty

The Drew Carey Show

"The Tell-Tale Heart"

Capitalize the first and last words and all the "important" words in between. Do not capitalize the "unimportant" little words, such as *a, the, to, of, for,* or *from,* which fall in the middle of a title. These words—known as "articles," "prepositions," and "connectives"—are not important when it comes to capitalization. Any other parts of speech (all the ones we went over in the last two lessons: nouns, pronouns, verbs, adjectives, and adverbs) are important and should be capitalized no matter how short they are. For example,

Frog and Toad Are Friends (book)

The Thin Red Line (movie)

Now, try a few more questions about Carter's draft on your own.

5 In sentence 18, how would <u>Grampa Gino's, Biddy's bagels,</u> be correctly written?

 A grampa Gino's, Biddy's bagels,

 B Grampa Gino's, Biddy's Bagels,

 C Grampa Gino's, biddy's bagels,

 D As it is

6 In sentence 22, how would <u>International Night, and the prom.</u> be correctly written?

 F International night, and the prom.

 G Internationel Night, and the prom.

 H international night, and the Prom.

 J As it is

7 In sentence 23, how would <u>Saturdays and Sundays visiting Colleges,</u> be correctly written?

 A saturdays and sundays visiting colleges,

 B Saturdays and Sundays visitting Colleges,

 C Saturdays and Sundays visiting colleges,

 D As it is

ANSWER KEY

1 C Spelling. Change the *y* to *i* before adding *-s*. The word *eatery* becomes *eateries*. Spot the misspelling in the question and look for the correct spelling among the answers. Use POE to eliminate any answers that do not contain *eateries*.

2 F Spelling. Change an unaccented *y* to *i* before adding *-ly*. The word *happy* becomes *happily*. After guessing aggressively that your answer will contain *happily*, cross off any choices that do not offer that spelling.

3 A Spelling. This one requires looking back at the passage. There you find that you need a word to indicate the owners of these minds. *Whose* is possessive; *who's* is short for *who is*.

4 J Spelling. Don't confuse *whether/weather* or *accept/except*.

5 B Capitalization. Capitalize the name of a business, Biddy's Bagels (but don't capitalize just any old bagels).

6 J Capitalization. International Night is the name of a particular night, while the prom is a type of dance. Notice how well POE works here. Suppose you know that International Night is capitalized but you aren't sure about prom. You can still eliminate **F** (night isn't capitalized), **G** (Internationel is a misspelling), and **H** (international night isn't in caps).

7 C Capitalization. Capitalize names of days of the week and *particular* colleges (like the College of William and Mary).

LESSON 7
MECHANICS: PUNCTUATION

PUNCTUATION

PERIODS

Use a period at the end of a sentence. We knew you knew that, but the tricky part, of course, is figuring out whether you *have* a sentence. Remember what we said in Lesson 4 about how a complete sentence needs a subject and a verb?

Incorrect: Making tamales with family members.

There is no subject, therefore no sentence. Who is making tamales? This is one of those "fragments" we told you to avoid at all costs. Whenever you have a "sentence" on the EOC exam beginning with an *-ing* word, check carefully. Chances are good it's a fragment.

Correct: Berthe Rivera is making tamales with family members.

Incorrect: Although this morning practice time may seem early.

There is no subject or verb here, leaving the reader with unanswered questions. *Although this morning practice time seems early, who* does *what*? If you can't answer those questions, chances are you're dealing with a sentence fragment.

Correct: Although this morning practice time may seem early, most swimmers on the varsity team are able to get up before dawn and into the water by 5:00 A.M.

Incorrect: Some scientists regard termites not as simple pests. But as intriguing subjects for research.

You usually don't start a complete idea with a word such as *but,* do you? Then don't set the second idea, above, off from the rest of the sentence with a period.

Correct: Some scientists regard termites not as simple pests, but as intriguing subjects for research.

Figuring out where one sentence ends and the next begins can be tricky too.

Incorrect: I'll wear my father's old tuxedo the prom is only three hours away.

This is actually two sentences that are mistakenly run together, hence called a "run-on" or "fused sentence." To fix it, throw in a period between the two complete ideas (each with its own subject and verb). Then read each resulting sentence aloud and see if it makes sense by itself.

Correct: I'll wear my father's old tuxedo.

That makes sense. I (subject) will wear (verb).

Correct: The prom is only three hours away.

That makes sense too. The prom (subject) is (verb).

Use a period after abbreviations. An abbreviation is a shortened form of a word: Mt., U.S., Ave., St., Dr., Ms., Mr.

When you use an abbreviation, you need to stick in a period (.) to show that you've left out some letters.

ABBREVIATIONS

United States	U.S.
Mount McKinley	Mt. McKinley
Green Street	Green St.
Doctor Didley	Dr. Didley

COMMAS

You're bound to find some questions on comma errors on the EOC English: Writing exam. Sometimes the exam makers will add a comma where none is necessary to see if you can spot the error. Other times they leave a required comma out to see if you miss it.

Use a comma to separate items in a series.

The refrigerator is filled with old bottles, bowls, and cartons.

Use a comma to separate two complete ideas in a sentence when they are separated by *and, or,* or *but.* A complete idea is one that could stand on its own as a sentence because it expresses a whole idea. It has both a subject and a verb.

I saw that I had a good chance to score, and the defender knew that she'd better act quickly.

The swelling on my ankle is better now, but it will be a neat trick getting my soccer cleat back on.

I could try cramming it in with all of my might, or I could just put on a sock and go shoeless.

Note: Do *not* use a comma to separate phrases joined by *and* or *or* if the phrases are not complete ideas.

Incorrect: He ate all the ice cream, and returned the box to the freezer.

The words *returned the box to the freezer* can't stand alone as a complete idea, can they? No! The subject—the "who"—is missing, so you should not add a comma.

Correct: He ate all the ice cream and returned the box to the freezer.

Interrupters

Don't you hate it when people keep interrupting you before you finish speaking? Well, as a writer you will meet "interrupters," too—nonessential words that separate subject and verb in a sentence. You can restrain them, though, by fencing them off with commas—one before and one after.

We called these interrupters "gobbledy-gook" when we were discussing subject-verb agreement. If the gobbledy-gook is *not* necessary to the meaning of the sentence, you should set it off with commas.

Uncle Jerry, *whose hair was thinning,* disliked being compared to a bald eagle.

The words, *whose hair was thinning,* are not really essential to the sentence about Uncle Jerry because the sentence would still make sense without them. The sentence still conveys the main point—that Uncle Jerry disliked the comparison—whether or not it tells you about his own balding head.

By contrast, the words, *whose hair is thinning,* are essential to the meaning of the following sentence and are *not* set off by commas.

Any man *whose hair is thinning* should smear sunscreen on his head.

If you take the phrase *whose hair is thinning* out, the sentence no longer conveys what it is supposed to. Instead, it sounds as if the writer wants *all* men to apply sunscreen on top—which is not at all what the writer means.

Appositives

Use commas to set off appositives from the rest of the sentence.

Boomerang, my crazy cat, sits on my keyboard.

Sometimes one word or phrase follows another and both refer to the same thing. That nonessential word or phrase is called an *appositive* and is set off from the rest of the sentence by commas. *Boomerang* and *my crazy cat* are interchangeable; they refer to the same thing. The words, *my crazy cat*, could be left out of the sentence and it would still mean the same thing: Boomerang sits on my keyboard.

Now see if you can figure out where the commas go in this sentence.

Michael Jordan NBA superstar retired in 1999.

Correct: Michael Jordan, NBA superstar, retired in 1999.

Use a comma to set off a nonessential word or phrase that introduces the subject.

Yes, I heard what you said.

Sometimes a nonessential word or group of words is at the beginning of a sentence instead of in the middle. Such words include *yes, therefore, however,* and *in addition.* Separate that introductory word or phrase from the crucial part of the sentence with a comma.

Hey, watch what you're doing!

Mr. Holstein, I'm moving on to greener pastures.

Just Because

Remember those times when you need a comma . . . just because! These are times when comma use has become established by convention—by common practice over hundreds of years—such as between the day and year in dates and after various parts of a friendly letter. Note the commas in the following letter:

March 3, 2004

Dear Buddy,

How are things up there on Long Island? I wanted to give you the scoop on what's happening down here. . . .

Faithfully Yours,

Bill

Also, don't forget the commas that separate parts of an address. When an address appears in a sentence, use a comma to separate the street from the city and the city from the state. There is no comma between the state and zip code, though.

Joe Shmo lives at 1600 Jefferson Avenue, Centreville, VA 22020.

Notice that when a city and state address appear in a sentence, commas go around the state name on *both* sides.

I lived in San Francisco, California, before moving to Virginia.

Use a comma to separate a quote from the speaker.

"I have a report to do," Curtis said.

"You're no help," Curtis complained.

Curtis yelled, "I thought you were going to help me!"

Curtis asked, "Where are you?"

Note: It's exception time. You *don't* use a comma to separate the quote from the speaker when the speaker is named *after* his exclamation or question. Exclamation points and question marks don't take commas beside them.

"I thought you were going to help me!" Curtis yelled.

"Where are you?" Curtis asked.

Don't overuse commas. You may remember being taught to use a comma every time you "hear" a pause. Well, delete that memory file! If you stick in a comma every time there's a break, you'll have way too many commas in your writing. Here's a better way to decide whether you need a comma: When in doubt, leave it out! When there's a rule that covers it, put it in!

> **TIP:** The idea behind commas—or any punctuation marks—is to make the idea clearer. If you find a comma muddying up an idea—say interrupting the normal flow of thought—you probably should take it out.

Common Comma Mistakes

Do not use a comma **after** a word such as *but*. Only use the comma *before* a word like *but*—and only when the word separates two *complete* ideas that could each stand alone as a sentence.

Incorrect: Mike brushes his teeth every night but, Saturday and Sunday.

Correct: Mike brushes his teeth every night but Saturday and Sunday.

Incorrect: I want to go to the prom but, I don't want to spend money on a limo.

Correct: I want to go to the prom, but I don't want to spend money on a limo.

Do not use a comma before the word *and* or *or* when it does not separate two complete ideas.

Incorrect: I am going to wear an old dress, and buy a new coat.

Incorrect: She usually put her hair up, or tied it back.

TIP: A comma splice is a very common error—and one that you should avoid like the plague!

Do not use a comma instead of a period to separate two complete ideas. You may have heard your teachers call this type of run-on error a "comma splice" because it incorrectly "splices together" two complete ideas with a comma.

Incorrect: One of the season's biggest hurricanes is approaching, it should reach us tomorrow.

SEMICOLONS

One way to correct a comma splice is to use a semicolon (;) instead of a comma for separating two complete ideas.

Correct: One of the season's biggest hurricanes is approaching; it should reach us tomorrow.

Besides linking two complete ideas, semicolons can replace some of the commas in a sentence to avoid confusion.

Messy and Confusing. I would like to thank Mona, my wife, Desmond, my agent, Mumtaz, my dog, and Damien.

Improved, with Semicolon. I would like to thank Mona, my wife; Desmond, my agent; Mumtaz, my dog; and Damien.

COLONS

Use a colon to introduce a list. The colon can often be translated as *as follows* or *as a result* or *this list*.

Reuben went to the convenience store for the following: chips, salsa, soda, popcorn, pretzels, and antacid.

She had only one request: money.

Use the colon after the salutation of a business letter.

Dear Members of the Board of Education:

Dear Editor:

To Whom It May Concern:

> **TIP:** Complete ideas do not begin with connectors such as *and, or, but,* or *for.* If you have one of these connectors, you don't need a semicolon. On the other hand, semicolons do often go hand-in-hand with one of these words: *however, therefore, furthermore, nevertheless, thus.* If you see one of these words in the middle of a sentence on the writing exam, chances are good that they should follow a semicolon.

Be careful not to use a colon instead of a semicolon, or vice versa. When you see a semicolon, check to make sure that there is a complete idea on either side. When you see a colon, check to make sure that you can translate it as *as follows*.

Incorrect: Highlights of the show will include; a speech by the President, appearances by several celebrities, and a fireworks display near the Washington Monument.

Correct: Highlights of the show will include: a speech by the President, appearances by several celebrities, and a fireworks display near the Washington Monument.

Correct: I flunked algebra last year; however, I took it over in summer school and got an A.

> **TIP:** If you already have a bunch of commas littering up a sentence, consider using semicolons to separate major word groupings from minor ones.

Let's practice some questions that require you to apply what we've reviewed about use of periods, commas, semicolons, and colons. Flip back to Carter's draft on page 89.

1 In sentence 18, how would <u>students, who like to hit the road, may</u> be correctly written?

    A students who like to hit the road, may

    B students who like to hit the road. May

    C students who like to hit the road may

    D As it is

2 In sentence 18, how would <u>Dr Doolittle's Veggie Treats</u> be correctly written?

    F Dr Doolittles Veggie Treats

    G Dr Doolittle's Veggie Treats'

    H Dr. Doolittle's Veggie Treats

    J As it is

3 In sentence 22, how would <u>the class barbecue Winter Carnival,</u> be correctly written?

    A the class barbecue, Winter Carnival,

    B the class Barbecue Winter Carnival,

    C the class barbecue winter Carnival,

    D As it is

4 In sentence 25, how would <u>a time of enjoyment, and freedom.</u> be correctly written?

    F a time of enjoyment; and freedom.

    G a time of enjoyment and freedom.

    H a time of: enjoyment and freedom.

    J As it is

5 In sentence 26, how would <u>For many at Ogilvie each</u> be correctly written?

    A For many, at Ogilvie each

    B For many at Ogilvie, each

    C For many at ogilvie each

    D As it is

6 In sentence 28, how would <u>pressures however, we can't</u> be correctly written?

    F pressures, however we can't

    G pressures; however, we can't

    H pressures however we can't

    J As it is

Check the answer key on page 109 for the correct answers.

QUESTION MARKS

The tricky part isn't knowing when to use a question mark but instead, when *not* to use it.

Use a question mark to indicate a direct question. Questions usually start out: Who? What? When? Where? Why? or How?

Do not use a question mark after a statement *about* a question.

How do I look?	Arnold wondered how he looked.
Are there any jobs?	Hermione inquired whether there were any jobs.
What's the matter, Nelson?	Nelson's father asked him what was bothering him.

EXCLAMATION POINTS

Use exclamation points only to express strong feeling—especially excitement or anger.

Nonsense!

Don't you dare touch me!

Oh, my!

Gadzooks!

Boy!

> **TIP:** If you see: He exclaimed, "Blah de blah blah!" make sure an exclamation point is used. On the other hand, don't overuse them—and probably don't use them at all in your composition for the direct-writing component of the EOC English: Writing exam. The composition is a formal piece of writing. Exclamation points are usually reserved for more informal pieces, such as a friendly letter or a piece of conversation written in dialogue form. Even then, save exclamation points for times when you really want to indicate the speaker's excitement. Otherwise, they lose their punch.

APOSTROPHES

Use an apostrophe to show possession or belonging.

the bridge's shelter

the man's bald head

Henry's doughnuts

the plan's benefit

Thomas's locker

three countries' borders

When showing ownership with a word that already ends in -*s*, add apostrophe + *s* if the word is singular.

Thomas's locker

Add the apostrophe alone if the word is plural.

countries' borders

Sorry, but as usual, there are exceptions to the rule that you form the possessive case by using an apostrophe.

Some possessive words do not contain apostrophes.

The ticket is *mine*.

The popcorn is *yours*.

The cat used *its* paw.

The mascara is *hers*.

Whose wallet is this?

The fault is *theirs*.

The championship title is *ours*.

As with commas, *do not overuse apostrophes*. If you have just a plural noun—no ownership—skip the apostrophe.

Incorrect: The contest featured cheerleaders' from several schools.

Correct: The cheerleaders' uniforms are different this year.

Use an apostrophe to indicate the missing letters in a contraction.

I'll for "I will"

couldn't for "could not"

would've for "would have"

Notice that the apostrophe replaces the missing letters in the words above.

Some Contractions You Should Know

Am, Are and *Is*	I'm, you're, we're, they're, he's, she's, it's, who's, where's, what's, there's
Will	I'll, you'll, she'll, he'll, we'll, they'll
Would	I'd, you'd, he'd, she'd, we'd, they'd
Have	I've, you've, we've, they've
Not	isn't, aren't, wasn't, weren't, haven't, hasn't, doesn't, didn't, wouldn't, shouldn't, couldn't, can't, won't

QUOTATION MARKS

Use quotation marks for punctuating dialogue. We guarantee that at least one of the passages on the exam will contain dialogue.

Enclose quoted words—either spoken or written—between quotation marks. Make sure that you haven't included other words from the sentence. Put anything besides exact words outside the quotes. That includes question marks—unless the quote, itself, is a question.

Incorrect: He took one look at her and, "Asked how are you feeling?"

Correct: He took one look at her and asked, "How are you feeling?"

Do not use quotation marks for *indirect* quotations. Quotations are used only when the words in between are someone's *exact* words.

Incorrect: She said that "she felt much better after eating something."

Correct: She said that she felt much better after eating something.

Correct: He asked how she was feeling.

Correct: She said, "I feel much better now that I've eaten something."

Start a new paragraph every time a new speaker speaks, and remember to indent the first line of all paragraphs. (The EOC exam people also want you to know that

---

when you are typing paragraphs on a word processor, an alternative to indenting is to double space between paragraphs.)

Igor shouted, "You're up, Thor!"

Thor cried out, "I can't find my lucky bat. You know I can't play with any other bat! It's the one I always use."

Igor said, "You call that your *lucky* bat?" Igor then turned and walked away.

Use quotes for titles. Put quotes around short works like the names of poems, lessons, magazine or newspaper articles, particular episodes of TV shows, and short plays.

"Why Can't You Behave?"	(song)
"Breaking the Code"	(lesson of book)
"Recycling Girl Scout Cookies"	(magazine article)
"Capitals Rally to Tie Hurricanes"	(newspaper article)
"Saturday's Primary"	(episode of radio show *The Diane Rehm Show*)
"Joey's Big Break"	(episode of TV program—*Friends*)
"The Raven"	(poem)
"The Tell-Tale Heart"	(short story)

Important note: When you are writing your EOC exam composition out by hand, you should use <u>underlining</u> to indicate the names of *whole* books, magazines, newspapers, and *long* plays. Italics—*slanted print like this*—are often used instead of underlining to indicate the name of a long piece. Now that computers and word processors practically rule the print world of books, newspapers, etc., you are more likely to see italics than underlining. Still, when you write something out by hand—as when you do your written composition for the EOC English: Writing Exam—you'll need to know when to underline.

<u>To Kill a Mockingbird</u> (book)

<u>Time</u> (magazine)

<u>Hamlet</u> (full-length play)

Try these questions about Carter's draft on page 89.

7 In sentence 22, how would <u>alot of group activities</u> be correctly written?

    A a lot of group activities

    B alot of group activities'

    C alot of group's activities

    D As it is

8 In sentence 24, how would <u>four years of coping with stress, many</u> be correctly written?

    F four years' of coping with stress, many

    G four years of coping with stress many

    H four years of copeing with stress, many

    J As it is

9 In sentence 27, how would <u>hold new pressure's too</u> be correctly written?

    A hold new pressure's too!

    B hold knew pressure's too.

    C hold new pressures too.

    D As it is

10 In sentence 29, how would <u>Iv'e come to realize that we really have nothing except</u> be correctly written?

    F I've come to realize that we really have nothing except

    G Iv'e come to realize that; we really have nothing except

    H Iv'e come to realize that we really have nothing accept

    J As it is

11 In sentence 31, how would <u>Wasn't it the poet Robert Herrick</u> be correctly written?

   A Was'nt it the poet Robert Herrick

   B Wasn't it the poet, Robert Herrick,

   C Wasn't it the poet, Robert Herrick

   D As it is

12 In sentence 31, <u>said "Gather ye rosebuds while ye may"</u>? be correctly written?

   F said, "Gather ye rosebuds while ye may"?

   G said "Gather ye rosebuds while ye may?"

   H said "Gather ye rosebuds while ye may."

   J As it is

Check the answer key on page 109 for the correct answers.

So far, you've reviewed the rules for grammar, usage, and mechanics that might be tested on the EOC English: Writing exam, *and* you've practiced doing multiple-choice items like those you'll see on the exam. All that's left is to prepare for the direct-writing portion, which we'll do in Lessons 9–12.

ANSWER KEY

1 C Commas. Use commas to set off *nonessential* phrases. In this case, "who like to hit the road" is essential. The writer isn't talking about all students—just those who like to hit the road and drive around.

2 H Periods. Use a period to indicate where letters have been removed from titles like Dr., Mr., Ms., M.D., or M.A.

3 A Commas. Use commas to separate items in a series.

4 G Commas. Don't overuse commas. A series would be three or more items. You don't need a comma to separate only two items.

5 B Commas. Use a comma to set off an introductory phrase from the main part of the sentence.

6 G Semicolons. Use a semicolon to link two complete ideas. The semicolon is often *followed* by a word, such as *however, therefore,* or *thus.*

7 A Apostrophe/Spelling. The word *activities* is a plural—not a possessive— and needs no apostrophe, so cross off **B**. There is no such word as *alot*, so eliminate **C** and **D**.

8 J Commas. Remember that in about one out of four of the questions where "As it is" is an option, "As it is" will be the correct answer! In this case, a comma is properly used—here, to set off the introductory phrase from the subject (many).

9 C Apostrophes. All you need to do is spot the error in the original and zoom in on the choice that corrects it. The word should be *pressures* (plural, not possessive). Don't waste time on any choices that contain the original error (**A, B,** and **D**).

10 F Apostrophes. The word *I've* stands for *I have.* Make sure that the apostrophe is positioned where the missing letters would be.

11 D Apostrophes. The contraction *Wasn't* is punctuated properly since the apostrophe replaces the missing letters (Was not). The poet's name is essential to the poem since the question would make no sense without it, so we don't set that name off with commas.

12 F Commas. Remember to punctuate dialogue correctly. When phrases like "he said" or "she said" come before the direct quote, put a comma before the quotation marks.

WRITING THE ESSAY

LESSON 8
WRITING THE ESSAY:
WRITING PROMPTS AND SCORING

Finally, the moment you've all been waiting for . . . We are about to unveil the secrets behind the writing prompt on the EOC English: Writing Exam. The prompt might be a question, an issue, or a hypothetical ("what-if") situation. And along with the prompt, remember that you'll get a handy checklist of things to keep in mind as you write (see pages 124–125). You will then have as long as you need to complete a piece of writing based on that topic.

Let's look at some sample prompts to get a feel for what the test makers will ask you to write about.

THE THREE KINDS OF PROMPTS

Questions:

What is the biggest problem at your high school?

What is the most important choice you have made in your life?

Issues:

Should there be a moment of silence in Virginia schools each morning?

Should public schools adopt school uniforms?

Hypothetical Situations:

Imagine that you woke up to discover that you were invisible. Describe your day.

Pretend that you have been elected president. What is the first action you would take?

HOW YOU'RE GRADED

At least two people will read and score your paper. You should keep those graders in mind as you write your masterpiece. Think of the mountains of compositions these guys have to review. The handwriting is often impossible to read, and the ideas are often so jumbled that they have *no idea* what students are attempting to convey. Hard to expect a high score in that situation, right?

Just think how much these graders must appreciate a paper that is legible and seems to follow a plan. Here's how the grading system works:

DOMAINS

First, they will read your writing pretty quickly and come to an overall impression.

Based on that impression, they each give your paper a score of 1 (low) to 4 (high) for each of what they call three "domains." These domains consist of "composing," "written expression," and "usage and mechanics." Your score for each domain is the total of the score assigned by both readers, with a total possible score of 6–24.

The scorers will not be looking for one "correct" response to the prompt. After all, you are supposed to be giving your personal ideas and supporting your own opinions. On the other hand, they don't just pull your score out of a hat. They will be looking for an answer that is clearly stated, amply supported, well organized, and grammatically correct. Give them what they want.

When they read your composition, the scorers want to see that you have mastered skills in the three areas we just mentioned. Here is a brief explanation of each of these "domains."

- **Composing** refers to your ability to put together a piece of writing that hangs together and conveys one central idea.

- **Written expression** refers to your skill at using language to communicate your purpose and tone.

- **Usage and mechanics** refers to your knowledge of correct grammar, capitalization, punctuation, and spelling.

SCORING

Composing

Score 1 Point: These are compositions that just don't cut it. In many of them the student doesn't address the writing prompt and doesn't do much planning before writing. There is hardly any support, and it looks as if the writer struggles to fill the page. The result is either a very short paper, or a longer one full of repetition and other padding, neither of which discusses the main idea of the writing prompt.

Score 2 Points: These head in the right direction, but don't go far enough. They "pass" because the writer did try to follow the directions in the writing prompt, but the papers are often lacking in specifics and organization. They usually have an opening and a closing, but not a lot of logical support for the main idea in between.

Score 3 Points: These are pretty good attempts to build a paper that does what the prompt asks. There is a plan for presenting the ideas in a logical order and transitions that make that plan apparent. The central idea is clear. There is plenty of support for it—examples, reasons, illustrations, etc.—and there are few irrelevant tangents. There is an introduction and a conclusion—perhaps not brilliant, but they work.

Score 4 Points: These papers are the polished ones. The writer has done what the writing prompt says to do, and has done it with some flair. The position is stated and clearly supported, and the tone is appropriate for the audience specified in the prompt. These are the papers that are not only pretty much error-free (although there may be a few errors in spelling, capitalization, and punctuation), but truly strong. They start with an intro that captures the reader's attention. They stick to the point with appropriate transitions to help readers follow the organized flow. They end with a conclusion that is more than just a summary of what's already been said—an ending that leaves the reader with a sense of why the author wrote this piece.

Written Expression

Score 1 Point: When it comes to word choice and sentence variety, there is none. These papers are awkward and monotonous and usually not much fun to read.

Score 2 Points: The use of language in these papers is pretty weak. Sentences are pretty blah with lots of general words and not much sentence variety. Sometimes the writer's meaning isn't clear. Occasionally the writer uses specific words or manages to include a few sentences that flow within an otherwise choppy sea of words.

Score 3 Points: The message is pretty clear. The writer makes careful word choices most of the time, and sometimes even employs language that is quite vivid. For the most part, sentences are varied and flow smoothly.

Score 4 Points: These are the memorable papers, the ones with style. You can "hear" the writer's distinctive voice through his or her use of precise, evocative language, and the piece has a rhythmic flow.

Usage and Mechanics

Score 1 Point: There are so many grammatical and spelling errors it's very hard to tell what this writer is trying to say.

Score 2 Points: These papers contain a lot of errors—especially in spelling and punctuation—and it's pretty hard to follow the writer's train of thought.

Score 3 Points: There aren't many errors, and when there are, they aren't the basic, common ones—and they generally don't obstruct the writer's message.

Score 4 Points: Although there may still be a few errors, they don't interfere with the reader's ability to understand what the writer is saying. This paper is almost flawless in terms of capitalization, punctuation, spelling, usage, and sentence formation.

Okay, so what does all of this mean in plain English? How do you write a paper that scores a 4 instead of a 1? Let's start with something simple—what the graders see (literally) when they look at your paper.

VISUAL APPEARANCE

How your composition looks—totally aside from what it says—matters.

Length: You are given four lined pages for your written composition. Your composition should just about fill those four pages. Sure, there are students who have gotten a "4" by writing less. But if the scorers see a really short essay, they may think you skimped on ideas.

Penmanship: You are given scratch paper on which to practice for the direct-writing component. You should use this paper to plan and compose your first draft. Be as messy as you want here, because this is for your eyes only. However, when it comes time to write your final draft on the lined pages you are given for your finished composition, you do need to write neatly.

The scorers have neither the time nor the inclination to put much energy into reading messy handwriting (or even big, neat, loopy lettering that's hard to read). You could be a future Pulitzer Prize winner, but the scorers will never see that if your handwriting is scribbly and full of cross-outs or otherwise hard on the eyes.

Re-reading favorite
novels is like
visiting old friends

Pretend you are a composition scorer. Which one looks like it has been written by somebody who's floundering and wants to hurry up and get this over? Which one looks like a high school student who knows what he or she wants to say and deserves a top score for the way he or she says it?

Margins: The lined paper has clear margins where each line begins and ends. Try not to run over these and try to start each line in about the same place.

EXAMPLE OF RAGGED MARGINS

Dear Editor:
I would like to state my opinion about banning smoking in public places. It is against our rights.
A lot of businesses would lose money if they did not allow their customers to smoke.
Smoking can make you sick, but that is your own business. It is true that some people who breathe your smoke might get sick too.

EXAMPLE OF STRAIGHT MARGINS

Dear Editor:
I am for banning smoking in public places. While many people are against the ban, I feel that the reasons for such a ban far outweigh the reasons against it. Smoke is hazardous to human health, harmful to the environment, and aesthetically displeasing. The main reason I support the ban is because smoking is detrimental to the health of smokers and those around them who are forced to breathe second-hand smoke . . .

Dear Editor:

I would like to state my opinion about banning smoking in public places. It is against our rights. A lot of businesses would lose money if they did not allow their customers to smoke. Smoking can make you sick, but that is your own business. It is true that some people who breathe your smoke might get sick too.

Sincerely,

Pete Pigpen

Dear Editor:

I am for prohibiting smoking in public places. While many people are against the ban, I feel that the reasons for such a ban far outweigh the reasons against it. Smoke is hazardous to human health, harmful to the environment, and generally unpleasant.

The main reason I support the ban is because smoking is detrimental to the health of smokers and those around them who are forced to breathe second-hand smoke.

Sincerely,

Nan Neatnik

Which composition looks as if it has been written by somebody who has an organizational plan and has put every idea in its place?

Which one looks as if it has been written by somebody who hasn't taken the time to put things in any logical order—and who probably hasn't cleaned up his or her room since the last millennium? Now, all of these assumptions may very well be *wrong*. Ms. Neatnik may not really have much of an organizational strategy. Mr. Pigpen may have written a brilliantly developed and organized response. The scorers may or may not detect this. If you're Pigpen, do you want to risk it? Not for something as easy to correct as legible handwriting and neat margins!

It's probably not a good idea to stick additions or changes in the margins, either. The scorers probably won't read them.

Obvious Paragraphs: So you've used neat handwriting and kept inside the margins. There's one more thing that you can do to make this composition reader-friendly and that is . . . indent, indent, indent.

The whole idea of a paragraph is to make things easier for the reader. You indent at the beginning of a paragraph to signal, "Hey, Reader! I'm shifting gears now." All of the ideas in this paragraph are about the same main thing. That main thing is different from that of the preceding paragraph and that of the following paragraph.

The indent—a nice big indent of at least half an inch—also makes things easier on the reader's eyes. Instead of one big blob of words, offer your reader nice manageable bites of three to five sentences each.

SUMMARY

- Try to fill up most of the pages provided.

- Make sure your handwriting is readable.

- Stay within the margins.

- Indent your paragraphs.

Now on to the meat of the matter—the ideas in your composition.

LESSON 9
WRITING THE ESSAY: SIX STEPS FOR WRITING ANY COMPOSITION

Remember how the multiple-choice portion of the exam will ask you questions about the writing processes of fictional students? In the direct-writing part of the exam, you need to have a clear idea of the writing process you, too, will follow. You can be sure you will write a better essay for the EOC English: Writing exam and any other assignment if you take these six steps.

1. **Understand the topic.** Read the topic very closely! Try putting it in your own words. This is your roadmap. If you read it wrong, you're lost. That means you have to keep in mind *what* you are saying, *why*, and to *whom*, every step of the way.

2. **Brainstorm ideas.** In Lesson 3, we talked about some ways to get the ideas flowing—discussing, listing, clustering, etc. Don't worry about complete sentences or spelling at this point, just think of as many ideas as possible.

3. **Organize the main ideas.** List at least three main points you want to make. These big ideas will be mentioned in the introductory paragraph. Then, each one will be developed in a paragraph of its own. Some people find it useful to start one of those traditional outlines we talked about in Lesson 3.

4. **Organize supporting details.** Under each main idea, place related reasons, examples, explanations, or illustrations. If you're using a traditional outline to organize these, they are lettered like this, remember?

   I.

      A.

      B.

      C.

   II.

      A.

      B.

      C.

Depending on your purpose, you might choose another way to organize your ideas, such as a chart that compares pros and cons in a particular debate, or a numbered timeline that shows the order in which certain events happened. You'll see several alternative organizers when you do the practice exams in Lessons 13 and 15.

5. **Plan your conclusion.** Decide on an ending thought for your composition. That thought should make your intent in writing this whole thing clear. An adequate ending would be one that summarizes what you've said and also answers the questions, "So what? Why does all of this matter?"

    You don't have to settle for an "okay" ending, though. Try connecting the beginning to the end in a memorable way. This is your last chance to make the impression you wish on your reader! We'll talk about how to write a jazzy, more-than-adequate conclusion later.

6. **Put your plan into action.** Using the ideas you have jotted down and organized, write the first draft of your composition on your scratch paper. Be a word thief and take some of the key words from the prompt for your introduction. If the prompt asks your opinion on school uniforms, for example, your introduction should contain the words *school uniforms.* Put the details you listed into complete sentences. Use some of those transition words we talked about in Lesson 4 (*First, Then, Most important,* etc.) to form connections between ideas. You should end up with an introductory paragraph, at least three body paragraphs, and a concluding paragraph. Each paragraph should be about the same length.

> **TIP:** Don't forget to transfer this draft to the lined paper, using legible handwriting!

Now let's go over all this in more detail, with specific writing prompts in mind. We'll start with a piece of persuasive writing, because that's the kind that's emphasized in Virginia in the eleventh grade.

Oscar found this prompt on the exam.

> **What is your position on "zero tolerance"—a strict school-discipline policy that punishes anyone who breaks any rules, big or small? Write to the school board about your position and explain your reasons for it.**

Using the steps above, let's help Oscar get started.

1. **Understand the topic.** Read the prompt carefully. He is supposed to tell the *school board* how he feels about the zero tolerance, "get tough," discipline policy.

2. **Brainstorm ideas.** Now is the time to stay loose as a goose. Let those creative juices flow. Brainstorm. Get down as many reasons as possible. Don't stop to decide which ones are "good" and which ones aren't, yet. Definitely don't worry *at this point* about writing in full sentences or correcting spelling errors.

   He may hate zero tolerance. He may love it. He may think that zero tolerance is okay for some schools but not others. The important thing is to choose a position and think of as many ways as possible to support that position.

   Oscar decides he hates zero tolerance and has to persuade the school board to hate it, too. He lists all the "cons" he can during this step.

3. **Organize main ideas.** Here are the main reasons Oscar comes up with for his opinion against zero tolerance.

   • Creates need for increased security technology

   • Causes higher drop-out rates

   • Increases alienation and negative attitude

Olivia, another test taker, has a different opinion of the zero-tolerance discipline policy. Look at the reasons she comes up with in favor of it.

   • Eliminates troublemakers

   • Prevents potential violence

   • Sends a clear message

4. **Organize supporting details.** Oscar jots down these examples, explanations, and effects to support each reason. Notice how he has used the traditional outline form. His three main ideas are the three reasons against the zero-tolerance policy. Each of these will be expanded into a topic sentence—one that gives the main idea—for a separate paragraph in the body of his letter.

   I. Increased school security technology

      A. Metal detectors and video cameras don't help

      B. Money spent on security technology could be better used for other school needs

      C. High-tech security creates a cold atmosphere in school

   II. Higher drop-out rates

      A. Suspension is not a punishment

      B. Students more likely to drop out after suspension

C. Drop-outs contribute to crime

III. Increased alienation and negative attitude toward school

    A. Because punishment doesn't fit the crime

    B. Because some unfairly targeted

    C. Sense of being an outsider hurts everyone

If you have more reasons, you may have more body paragraphs. That's fine.

5. **Plan the conclusion.** Oscar thinks about how to finish off his composition with a short paragraph that tells what he said and why it matters. He summarizes his position and reminds his reader what he wants that reader to do.

- Against zero tolerance policy because of increased security technology, drop-out rates, and negativity toward school

- Wants the reader not to support this policy

6. **Put the plan into action.** Oscar now does two final things.

The Big Thing: He takes his organized ideas and expands the phrases into complete sentences. On this first draft—written on scratch paper—he makes as many erasures and cross-outs as he wants.

The Smaller Thing: He goes back and fine-tunes his letter to make it as good as it can be before writing the final copy on the lined pages he has been given at the beginning of the exam session. That means he

- looks for places where he can add more specific details that support and explain what his general ideas mean

- adds some more details or examples that help readers "see" in their mind's eye what he is describing

- replaces boring, ho-hum words like "nice" or "want" or "get" with more effective, precise words and expressions like "enthusiastic" or "value" or "collect"

- checks that all the paragraphs are about the same length

- polishes the conclusion and makes it shine

- adds any other finishing touches that provide a sense of order and completeness

- proofreads it for errors.

At this point, all that review of grammar, usage, and mechanics rules that he did with us in Lessons 5–8 should pay off!

OSCAR'S ESSAY

Here's Oscar's final masterpiece—the one that ends up on the lined pages in the exam booklet.

Dear Members of the School Board:

Violence in our schools is a serious problem that we cannot afford to ignore, but I am not in favor of zero tolerance. Such a policy creates at least three problems: an increase in expensive security technology, a rise in the student drop-out rate, and a growing sense of alienation among students. I am writing to explain my position that zero tolerance does not work and to ask your support for a policy that gets at the root of the problem.

First, zero-tolerance policies across the nation have brought a sharp increase in school security technology. Metal detectors and video surveillance are costly, and there is very little hard evidence that they really increase school safety. The money would be much better spent on hiring more teachers, buying more books, and renovating dilapidated schools. Besides the cost, there is the risk of actually escalating the problem. Schools that put metal detectors and police officers at the door may create a more negative climate and contribute to a vicious cycle: greater alienation, more fear, more violence.

Second, get-tough disciplinary measures result in more teenagers dropping out of school. Many students do not consider it much of a punishment to be forbidden to attend school. Studies show that students who drop out in the end are more likely to have been punished by suspension than those who stay in school. As the number of students who are suspended and expelled goes up, the crime rate in the community multiplies. Is this what we really want?

Third, and perhaps most important, zero-tolerance policies increase students' general sense of alienation. Strict zero tolerance has resulted not only in confiscation of weapons but in expulsion for possession of everything from cough drops to nail files.

Students who experience or even observe severe punishment that does not "fit the crime" resent the injustice. They often experience a general sense of disconnection from school.

If they perceive that certain groups of students seem to be punished more severely for less serious offenses, their sense of alienation and anger may be even greater. One of the lessons we should have learned by now is that such alienation hinders the individual from learning, creates a negative academic environment for students overall, and may even have tragic consequences for society.

In conclusion, I hope that you will see that a zero-tolerance policy is not the answer and does not work. There is no doubt that schools need to respond to minor incidents before they result in serious violence, but zero tolerance is often an over-reaction leading to no solution. Rather, we need to make sure the consequence is appropriate for the misbehavior—and to come up with safety plans that prevent the need for punishment in the first place. I ask that you do everything in your power to see that instead of kicking more students out of our schools, we try to find better ways of keeping more of them in.

Sincerely,

A Concerned Student

CHECKLIST

Here's a checklist like the one you will find on the same page as your writing prompt when you take the direct-writing section of the EOC exam.

Use it to evaluate "Concerned Student's" letter.

___ Did the writer plan and organize the paper before writing it?

Did the writer revise the paper to include

___ an attention-getting introduction?

___ plenty of specific supporting evidence for the central idea?

___ only ideas that support that main idea?

___ sentences and paragraphs that follow a logical order?

___ sentences that are clear, varied, and smooth-flowing?

____ vocabulary that conveys a tone appropriate for the writer's audience and purpose?

____ a conclusion that offers a wrap-up without just saying the same thing again?

Did the writer edit the paper to make sure that

____ grammar is correct?

____ capitalization is correct?

____ fragments and run-ons are eliminated?

____ misplaced modifiers are put in the right place?

____ spelling is error-free?

Did the writer go over the paper to ensure that

____ his or her purpose in writing the paper is clearly communicated?

____ the paper accomplishes what it is supposed to?

SCORE OSCAR'S ESSAY

Here's a chart that gives you the chance to play scorer.

Composing	____/4 points
Written Expression	____/4 points
Usage and Mechanics	____/4 points
TOTAL:	____/12 points

If we were one of the scorers, we'd give the essay a score of 12 points, which means a top score of 4 in all three domains. Wouldn't you?

Oscar seems to have had no problem figuring out a logical way to organize his ideas, but what if you aren't so lucky? What if you breeze through steps 1 and 2 (understanding the topic and brainstorming ideas)—then have no idea what to do next?

Let's talk about how to "put your house in order."

LESSON 10
WRITING THE ESSAY: STRUCTURE

This may sound funny, but on the EOC English: Writing Exam—and on many other essay tests—*how* you say things is as important as *what* you say. The scorers may not care much about the exact kind of house you build, but they want it to be one that is well constructed. They want to look at the floor and the walls and the roof and see that everything is put sturdily together.

Suppose the writing prompt asks you to give your opinion of changing to a year-round school schedule. The scorers probably don't care much whether you're for or against year-round school, but they really do want to see that you know how to come up with a plan for building a strong case with lots of detail. We're going to talk about how to make that plan obvious to the graders. A good EOC exam essay is one that is not only well put-together but also *obviously* well put-together.

PATTERNS OF ORGANIZATION

After you have brainstormed ideas on a particular topic, you need to decide how to arrange them logically. There are five basic types of organization you can use:

- **Time:** Organizes the description of events by the order in which they happened (or in the reverse order).

- **Space:** Organizes the description of the appearance of something from top to bottom or left to right.

- **Cause and Effect:** Organizes the description of linked events to show how one leads to another or was caused by another.

- **Comparing and Contrasting:** Organizes the description of two things so that their similarities and differences are provided.

- **Order of Importance:** Organizes ideas from the most important to the least important (or vice versa).

When to Use Patterns of Organization

- **Time:** To tell a story. To describe a series of events. To explain a procedure.

- **Space:** To tell how something looks. To describe the layout of a place. To explain where something is located.

- **Cause and Effect:** To explain why an event or a series of events occurred. To tell about the result of, or reason for an event or series of events.

- **Comparison/Contrast:** To describe one thing by reference to another. To argue that one thing is better (or worse) than another.

- **Order of Importance:** To give reasons for holding a certain position. To persuade a reader to accept your opinion.

Which type of organization you choose depends on your purpose for writing. Two people might use different organizational patterns to write on the same topic. One person might use more than one pattern at the same time. (Oscar used both order-of-importance and cause-and-effect when he wrote about zero-tolerance policies.)

PURPOSES

On the EOC English: Writing exam, you might be asked to write for one (or a combination) of purposes.

- to inform

- to explain

- to analyze

- to entertain

- to persuade

These are the purposes that are actually listed in the SOLs for Grades 9–11, and you're probably quite familiar with all of these from classroom assignments, but let's look at them using a scenario where you are throwing a party.

- **Informing:** When you write an invitation to a party, your goal is to *inform* people of the *who, what, when,* and *where* of the party.

- **Explaining:** When a friend calls for precise directions, you *explain* exactly *how* to get there by describing the route. When she asks why you are throwing the party, you *explain* your reasons *why.*

- **Analyzing:** When you plan the party, you *analyze* the *elements* that go into it by thinking about the separate parts that make it up (food, music, activities, etc.). When you *compare* the ways this party is like last year's or speculate on the *causes* of your last party's success, you are also *analyzing* it.

- **Entertaining:** When you tell a friend at the party a funny or interesting story about something that happened to you last week, your purpose is mainly to *entertain*.

- **Persuading:** When you spend an hour trying to convince your parents that they should let you have another party next month, your main goal is to *persuade* them.

As you can see, you might have two or more purposes for writing. For example, given the topic "How to Survive High School," you might have two purposes: to communicate real information to incoming freshmen, as well as to entertain them.

Consider this prompt.

Describe an important choice you made and explain why you made it.

Two different students might approach this prompt differently. One might decide to describe the chain of events that led to the decision. A cause-effect pattern of organization would be best for accomplishing his purpose. Another student might decide to list several reasons that came together in her decision. She might decide that her purpose would best be served by organizing her ideas by order of importance.

To understand your purpose, you need to think carefully about your topic. The following table makes some suggestions about how to do that:

FIGURING OUT YOUR PURPOSE IN WRITING

Ask yourself:	Purpose	Consider this organization first:
Am I telling a story?	To Entertain	Time
Am I telling the steps in a process?	To Inform	Time
Am I describing how a person, place, or thing looks?	To Inform	Space
Am I explaining why or how something happens?	To Analyze	Cause and Effect
Am I describing the similarities between two things?	To Analyze	Comparing Contrasting
Am I trying to convince my readers to accept my opinion?	To Persuade	Order of Importance

PRACTICE EXERCISE—PURPOSE

Here are some sample prompts. Think about what your *main* purpose in writing the response to each would be. Put one of the five purposes in each blank (inform, explain, analyze, entertain, persuade). Answers may vary. Check page 131 for suggested answers.

1 Should smoking be banned in all public places? _____

2 Write a short report on an endangered species. _____

3 Argue for why a particular TV program is worth watching. _____

4 Write a letter of inquiry requesting information that will help you write a report on cloning. _____

5 Write a humorous story about your most embarrassing moment. _____

6 Discuss how a historical event has affected your life today. _____

7 Write an article for incoming freshmen that tells the steps in a procedure they need to know. _____

8 Write a story about a courageous action you heard about or experienced. _____

9 Write a letter of complaint to a certain company telling why you are returning one of their products that you bought at a school fund-raiser. ──────────

10 Discuss the ways you and your best friend are alike and different. ──────────

11 Suggest how to prepare for the EOC English: Writing exam. ──────────

ANSWER KEY

PRACTICE EXERCISE: PURPOSE

1 persuade

2 inform

3 persuade

4 explain

5 entertain

6 analyze

7 inform

8 entertain

9 explain

10 analyze

11 inform

PRACTICE EXERCISE—SELECTING TYPE OF ORGANIZATION

Below are the writing prompts you considered in the last exercise. This time, consider the *type(s) of organization* you would use for each. (In many cases, two or more could work.) Put the name(s) of the organization in the blank: time, space, cause and effect, comparison/contrast, or order of importance.

Answers may vary. Check the answer key on page 133 for suggested answers.

1 Should smoking be banned in all public places? _____

2 Write a short report on an endangered species. _____

3 Argue for why a particular TV program is worth watching. _____

4 Write a letter of inquiry requesting information that will help you write a report on cloning. _____

5 Write a humorous story about your most embarrassing moment. _____

6 Discuss how a historical event has affected your life today. _____

7 Write an article for incoming freshmen that tells the steps in a procedure they need to know. _____

8 Write a story about a courageous action you heard about or experienced. _____

9 Write a letter of complaint to a certain company telling why you are returning one of their products that you bought at a school fund-raiser.

10 Discuss the ways you and your best friend are alike and different.

11 **Suggest how to prepare for the EOC English: Writing exam.** _____

(We suggest that you also write the responses to some of these 11 prompts—and others you find later in the lesson—for practice. Use the checklist on pages 124–125 guide and evaluate your writing.)

ANSWER KEY

PRACTICE EXERCISE: SELECTING TYPE OF ORGANIZATION

(Answers may vary)

1 order of importance, cause and effect

2 cause and effect, time, space

3 order of importance

4 cause and effect, time, space

5 time, cause and effect

6 cause and effect, time

7 time, space, cause and effect

8 time, cause and effect

9 cause and effect

10 order of importance, cause and effect, space

LESSON 11
WRITING THE ESSAY: THE WRITING FRAME, SUPPORTING DETAILS, AND CONCLUSIONS

THE WRITING FRAME

We already know the *format* of the writing prompt you will find on the EOC English: Writing Exam. It will be either a question, an issue, or a hypothetical situation, but we *can't* predict exactly what the prompt will ask you to do—or how you should organize your answer. To make up for that, we're going to give you another tool to put in your toolkit. We're going to give you writing frames you can use to help build a composition on *any* writing prompt topic, depending on which type of organization you choose. Change the frames as much as you like. Add to to them. Stretch them out.

ORDER OF IMPORTANCE

Sample Prompt

> **What do you think of requiring students in your school to wear identification badges?**
>
> **Write to the Board of Education and defend your position.**

1. The Introductory Paragraph

I am writing to persuade you that _____. My position is based on three reasons: _____, _____, and _____.

2. First Body Paragraph

The main reason for my position is _____.

This is the topic sentence for the paragraph. It explains the main idea of the paragraph. The rest of the paragraph will offer details that support that main idea by explaining the reason.

---

3. Second Body Paragraph

> Another reason for my position is _____.

This is the topic sentence for the paragraph. All of the other sentences in the paragraph explain the second reason with facts, details, examples, etc. Any sentence that does not somehow explain or clarify the main idea does not belong in the paragraph.

4. Third Body Paragraph

> A third reason for my position is _____.

This is the topic sentence elaborated by other supporting sentences in the paragraph.

5. Concluding Paragraph

> In conclusion, I believe that _____ because _____, _____, and _____. (If you want the reader to take a particular action:) I hope that I have persuaded you to _____.

This is the closing paragraph. It should summarize the main points found in the introduction and should give a sense of closure to the whole piece. In other words, it should convince the reader to adopt the writer's point of view!

In the answer key on page 147 you will find two finished sample letters based on the writing prompt about student IDs. Notice how the first letter was revised and improved.

Of course, the EOC prompt will not always require you to do a piece of persuasive writing, and you won't always be listing ideas in order of importance, so you can't always use this exact frame. The good news is, you can *adjust* the frame to work with just about any topic. Regardless of your purpose for writing a composition, the frame has the same basic parts:

- **Introduction** (in which you briefly tell your readers what you're about to tell them)

- **Body** (in which you go ahead and tell them—by developing one point per paragraph)

- **Conclusion** (in which you tell them what you've told them—and why it matters)

You adjust your frame mainly by varying the *transitions* you use in the body.

Let's look at a sample topic you might develop by cause and effect.

How would your life change if you won a million dollars?

Here's how you might frame the body of your composition.

First paragraph of the body: "If I won a million dollars, *one change* would be ..."

Second paragraph of the body: "A *second result* would be ..."

Third paragraph of the body: "A *third consequence* would be ..."

Here's a sample EOC topic you might write about using comparison/contrast:

How is science fiction different from realistic fiction? Which do you prefer?

The frame for your composition's body might look like this.

First paragraph of the body: "*While* science fiction ..., realistic fiction ...,"

Second paragraph of the body: "Science fiction ..., *but* realistic fiction ...,"

Third paragraph of the body: "*Although* science fiction ..., realistic fiction ...,"

The following is a sample topic that it would make sense to organize by time arrangement.

Describe the lifetime accomplishments of someone you admire.

Here's how you might frame the body.

First paragraph: "*By the time* Penelope Pfeffernussen was 20, she had
_____. *As soon as* she _____, she _____ ..."

Second paragraph: "*Later*, during middle age, she _____. *While* ...and *then* ... *Afterward*, she ..."

Third paragraph: "*Today* she ... She *still* ... She is *in the process* of ... and plans to ...*in the future*."

Last but not least, let's look at a topic that would lend itself well to spatial arrangement of ideas.

Write a short report on the geography of Thailand.

Here's one possible way of framing the body.

First Paragraph: "In the north ..."

Second Paragraph: "In the central region ..."

Third Paragraph: "In the south ..."

For all these frames, all you have to do in the conclusion is tie things up. Summarize your three or more body paragraphs and then end with a general comment such as

- what you want the Board of Education to do

- how you would feel about suddenly being a millionaire

- your attitude toward science fiction versus realistic fiction

- the impact that Penelope has had on you

- why it's important to know about Thailand's geography

Now that you have your frames in hand, let's talk more about how to flesh them out.

SUPPORTING DETAILS

We can't stress enough how important it is to *support* your ideas as you write your EOC exam composition. Don't just toss in a general reason unless you can explain it. Clarify the reason. Give plenty of details to support the reason. Feel free to drop some famous names here or quote some impressive statistics or facts to back up your position. Show the EOC exam scorers that you *know what you are talking about.*

In fact, using supporting details effectively is so important to a high score on the EOC written composition that we're going to give you some extra practice.

PRACTICE EXERCISE—ELABORATION
Let's take this writing prompt.

> **Some schools have decided to do away with student lockers. Write to your state senator about this issue. State your position and defend it.**

Here are three reasons that our friend Oscar gives in support of his position that high-school lockers should not be eliminated. Take each reason and *elaborate* with at least three more ideas that somehow clarify, explain, or illustrate it. (You are brainstorming, here, so don't worry about complete sentences. Cluster your ideas on another piece of paper if that would be helpful.)

Start thinking about how you'll arrange these ideas and what type of organization you should use. You might find cause-and-effect order helpful as you look at *how* lockers result in clutter reduction, comfort enhancement, and theft control. You might also use spatial arrangement as you order some of your ideas about what a cluttered locker or a comfortable student looks like! Then check and see how your elaboration compares with the samples in the answer key on page 150.

Reason 1: School lockers are necessary to prevent clutter.

-

-

-

Reason 2: Lockers make students more comfortable.

-

-

-

Reason 3: Lockers reduce theft.

-

-

-

Check the answer key on page 150 for sample responses.

STILL MORE PRACTICE—ELABORATION

Here are some general statements you might make in response to various writing prompts. In each case, supply three details (examples, reasons, facts, illustrations, etc.) that support each general statement.

I would be appropriate for class president because I am conscientious.

-
-
-

Grades should be abolished because they discourage creativity.

-
-
-

Passing the EOC exams should be a graduation requirement because it tests skills every graduate needs.

-
-
-

A school dress code is important because it helps create a positive learning environment.

-
-
-

Check the answer key on pages 150–151 for some sample answers.

THE CONCLUSION

We told you that you can write just an adequate conclusion for any composition. One that ends a persuasive piece might go like this:

> "In this letter I have defended my position that _____ because _____, and _____. I hope that you will now do everything in your power to _____."

Voila! You're finished, if you want to be. This isn't a slam-bang finish, but it does the job. You've summarized your key points in a nutshell. You've told your reader what you said.

Of course, you may want to jazz up your conclusion a bit. For a 4, graders like to see that you've really put some imagination and thought into the piece. There's no place like the conclusion for showing your reader that you have a flair for choosing striking words or finding vivid illustrations or coming up with an unusual perspective.

THE KICKER

Try doing what many good journalists do: End your piece with a "kicker." A kicker is a final thought that gives your reader something to think about. It's a thought that finalizes the whole piece. Sometimes it is a "rah-rah" call to action that vigorously answers the question, "So what do you want me to do about it?" Sometimes it is a humorous thought that makes your reader smile. Sometimes it's a catchy phrase.

It may well be a memorable line about how much better the world would be if only everyone took the position you have just defended. It may be a notable quote. It may be a look into the future. Whatever it is, it should answer the reader's question, "So what? Why did you spend all this time saying all this? What's the big deal? What's the main point you want me to remember when I've forgotten everything else you've said?"

After all, the last lines of your essay—in fact, the last part of almost anything we read—often ends up being the only part we recall. Make those lines memorable. Here are some examples of decent kickers. They don't just restate what has already been said. They indicate with feeling why it all matters, anyway, and what they want the reader to do about it.

Here are some examples.

> In conclusion, graduated licensing programs may limit driving freedom, but they reduce traffic deaths. Please vote for graduated licensing in our state and help save lives.

It is urgent that you use your influence to end the problem of overcrowding in our schools and that you do it now. Students literally deserve room to breathe!

We[students]have to take a stand against violence in public schools. Wearing a uniform is a small sacrifice to pay.

FINISHING TOUCHES

Now that you have the basics you need to score well on the essay, it's time to cover a few things that will help you polish our essay into one that is worthy of a 4 in each domain.

SPECIFIC WORDS

The scorers are looking for specific details and like to see you use precise words. This shows that you have good "control" of the language. In Lesson 4, we practiced answering multiple-choice questions that test your ability to identify better, more specific word choices a fictional student writer could have made.

Likewise, when you're the writer, you need to choose your words with care. Don't be satisfied with the first word that pops into your mind. Use the one that conveys *exactly* what you mean in the tone that you mean.

For example, don't settle for the usual verb, such as "going," when there's a more vivid one you can come up with. Replace those overused nouns and adjectives, like "guys" and "nice," with more striking ones. And be careful to choose the word that sets the right tone. (If you're writing an ad, would it sound better to call your product "cheap" or "moderately priced"?) Your more precise version may be longer than the original or it may be shorter.

Here are some examples of what we mean.

Blah and not very good. D'Marco *looked* at me.

More precise. D'Marco (*peered, glared, stared, glanced, scowled, beamed*) at me.

Blah. Here's a picture of Dee Dee *when she was younger.*

More precise. Here's a picture of Dee Dee *when she was younger, with dark brown curly hair, sporting a sleeveless top that reveals smooth, caramel-colored arms.*

Blah. *The Simpsons* is a *popular show.*

More precise. *The Simpsons* is a *highly profitable and successful television series.*

Remember: More precise *doesn't* necessarily mean longer.

> **Overly wordy.** It goes without saying that the coyote is never hurt, lamed, or wounded by the roadrunner.
>
> **More precise.** The roadrunner never injures the coyote.

TRANSITIONS

Here is a list of transitional devices you can use to make your essay flow smoothly.

Time—*after, as soon as, before, by the time, during, earlier, finally, first (second, third, etc.), last week (month, year), later, meanwhile, next, now, then, today, tomorrow, when, while, yesterday, today, in the future.*

Space—*above, among, around, below, beneath, beside, between, east, front, in back of, in the center of, near, next to, north, on the left side, on the right side, on top of, opposite, over, rear, south, under, upon, west.*

Cause and Effect

Cause—*as a result of, because, because of, caused by, since, the cause.*

Effects—*cause(s), consequently, result(s) in, so, therefore, the effect/result, thus.*

Comparison/Contrast

Comparison—*alike, also, both, common, equally, in the same way, just as, likewise, same, similar, too.*

Contrast—*although, but, differ, different, however, in contrast, on the other hand, unlike, whereas.*

Order of Importance—*above all, another reason, equally important/significant, finally, for one thing, less important/significant, the main reason, also, chiefly, even more important/significant, first (second, third, etc.), in addition, the least important (significant), the most important (significant).*

PRACTICE EXERCISE: WRITING A PERSUASIVE LETTER

Now put everything we've talked about in this lesson together as you write a letter in response to the following prompt. When you've finished putting the finishing touches on your letter, see how it compares with two scored sample letters found in the answer key on page 147.

The board of education is considering requiring all high-school students to wear identification badges while on school grounds. Write to the board explaining your opinion of such a requirement. Give reasons for your position and support your reasons.

The more writing you do between now and the actual exam, the better. Here are some more topics for writing practice. Since persuasive writing and business letters are both stressed in eleventh grade, we've included plenty of those. Who knows? One might even end up on the exam you take.

Describe your personal hero.

Explain why you are interested in a particular career.

Tell a story about surviving a disaster, based on something you heard about or experienced.

Write to an organization for up-to-date information on a topic you are researching.

Write a letter of application for a job you would like, telling why you should be hired.

Write a letter of complaint about a faulty product or an inadequate service.

Write a letter of request for a particular document, product, or action.

A new football stadium has been built in your state. Tell the team owner what you would like to see it named—and why.

In some states, teenage drivers are subject to harsher punishments for traffic violations than older drivers are. Write a letter to the editor of your local newspaper about whether you think the law should treat teenage drivers like older drivers.

Should teenagers be allowed to work more than ten hours a week? Write to your senator.

Many schools across the nation have a "service requirement." Students must complete a certain number of hours volunteering in order to get their high school diplomas. Write a speech to present to your parent-teacher organization in which you defend your position on the requirement.

Some schools have students take pre-prom breathalizer tests. Write to the president of your school board and state your position on this policy.

Some people feel that we need to require service in the armed forces. Write a letter to the president stating your position.

Write a letter to the editor of your local or school newspaper about your position on one of the following:

Should it be illegal to sell fur coats here made in other countries from dog fur?

What is your position on dress and hair codes for your high school?

Should school officials be able to check student lockers without student permission?

What do you think are appropriate penalties for driving drunk?

Some schools test all kids participating in after-school activities for drugs. What's your position?

Do you think having school uniforms in public high schools is a good idea?

How could the traffic in high-school hallways be improved?

What do you think is the worst problem in your school and what should be done about it?

What's your position on metal detectors and police security in high schools?

Should boxing be banned?

Should hunting be banned?

Should you save your pet's life no matter what the cost?

Should school start later in the day?

Should lie-detector tests be banned?

Should all high-school students in the United States have to pass the same test to graduate?

Should all Virginia students have to pass six EOC exams to graduate?

Why will you or won't you vote in the first presidential election for which you are eligible?

Try to convince someone why he or she should come to your hometown for a visit.

Argue for or against daylight savings time.

Is there anything wrong with "soap-opera addiction"?

Some people think there should be an end to "tracking"—placing students with similar skills and abilities together. What do you think?

And finally . . . good luck! You won't need it, though, because you have something even better: You have all the skills and preparation it takes to succeed on this test!

ANSWER KEY

PRACTICE EXERCISE: SAMPLE PROMPT—STUDENT BADGES (PAGE 135)

Sample Letter:

Dear Board of Education,

I am strongly for, that High School students should have to where ID badges. I feel badges make schools safer, for convenience, and for savings.

To start, badges it so you can see if someone belongs in the school. Badges are something many people hate the idea of. They think they look stupid. They need to remember that alot of people in the world are doing this. Alot of students in other schools are wearing them. Alot of businesses make people wear them also.

Badges can make things more convenient. Badges might be used as libary cards as one example. You need your student ID number if you get a book out of the libary. You have to go pull out that piece of paper out of your backpack every time you go. Badges would be more convenient. You could give the badge to the libarian and your number would be right on their.

Finally, this badge wouldn't cost hardly anything. A lot of other things cost a lot of money. Schools need all the money they can get. They need money for computers and video equipment. A lot of books in our libary are very old. Schools need money for new books even more than for computers. Other schools are spending a lot of money on expensive cameras and metal detecters. We should be glad if we only have to pay a little for student IDs. We should not complain when this badge can make your life safer.

Sincerely,

Oscar

Total Points Earned (by adding both scorers' scores on all three domains): 12

In this response, the position (for ID badges) is supported by three reasons (safety, convenience, and cost). However, the reasons are not well elaborated. The writing is wordy and repetitious—but low on specifics. Much of the writing is not persuasive. There is a limited control of written language—few specific words, no colorful language, no transitional devices, little variation in sentence structure. Several errors in spelling, capitalization, punctuation, and usage are made. Overall, this response presents enough information to be considered only minimally successful.

Let's look at a better letter on student ID's.

Dear Members of the Board of Education:

I am writing to express my support for the idea of requiring high school students to wear ID badges while in school. While many students hate the idea of wearing a security badge everywhere, I can think of many positives to outweigh the negatives. The badges should be adopted for reasons of safety, convenience, and cost-effectiveness. I have put a good deal of thought into the matter, and hope that when the time comes for you to take action on this matter, you will agree.

My main reason for supporting the requirement is that badges can enhance student safety by keeping intruders off campus. Certainly plenty of businesses and military installations have already discovered the utility of badges in strengthening security.

Critics of the badges point out that some of the most notorious cases of recent violence on school grounds has been committed by students at the school, not by outsiders. Granted, an ID badge requirement probably would not have averted these particular tragedies. Nevertheless, they would help prevent the more common but less visible types of trouble that arise when people who do not belong inside the building wander the halls at will. In order to keep outsiders from strolling around the school, it is necessary to use any effective means to ensure the safety of our students.

A second reason for requiring badges is that they may actually make life easier for students. Who says that wearing ID badges has to be such an inconvenience? If anything, an ID badge might facilitate various school-related activities. For example, principals around the county are considering placing a bar code on each badge. The coded badge could then be used for library check-outs, entrance to sports events, and even purchasing lunch. Who hasn't had the experience of getting ready to check out a book at the library and having to scrabble around in your backpack to find that paper with your student ID number that has sunk, naturally, to the very darkest recesses of the pack? Think how much easier it would be simply to hand your badge and get what you need.

Finally, student ID badges are cost-effective. Other school systems are spending thousands if not millions of dollars on security measures such as surveillance cameras, metal detectors, and mock lock-downs. How much does this potential library card/meal ticket/ mild security measure cost? Absolutely nothing. Members of the Board, I urge you to do everything in your power to see that the ID badge requirement is adopted. This badge can make students' lives both easier and safer without costing a dime.

Sincerely,

Oscar

Total Points Earned: 23

This fluent response is consistent and well organized, presenting three reasons (safety, convenience, and savings) why student ID badges should be required. Each reason is elaborated in depth with several specific details and examples. Careful, precise word-choice, use of appropriate transitional devices, and effective use of rhetorical devices (refuting the opposition, rhetorical questions) contribute to this composition's success. Finally, the writer shows good attention to his audience—the members of the board of education—from start to finish.

PRACTICE EXERCISE: ELABORATION (PAGES 138–139)

Remember that there are many possible answers for this exercise. Check our suggested answers to make sure you are on the right track.

Reason 1: School lockers are necessary to prevent clutter.

- classroom aisles—fire hazards

- getting around in already crowded hallways—even harder

- no place in cafeteria for backpacks

Reason 2: Lockers make students more comfortable.

- wearing coats and boots around in winter without lockers to put them in

- hard on our backs if we had to carry all our books around all the time

- some kids put mirrors, other personal items in lockers

Reason 3: Lockers reduce theft.

- sports equipment and musical instruments

- jackets that get left behind

- calculators

STILL MORE PRACTICE: ELABORATION (PAGE 140)

I would be appropriate for class president because I am conscientious.

- achieved straight As last semester in school

- never tardy, few absences from school

- finish what I start

Grades should be abolished because they discourage creativity.

- worried about good grades, less likely to take risk of expressing unusual ideas

- stressed out about grades, can't relax and let creative juices flow

- teachers—under pressure to turn in grades, less time for creative teaching

Passing the EOC exams should be a graduation requirement because they test skills every graduate needs.

- need writing skills—applications, college work, and on-the-job writing

- need reading skills—college classes, work-related reading

- need math, science, social studies—to be informed consumer, citizen

A school dress code is important because it helps create a positive learning environment.

- everyone looks same—more likely to treat each other as equals

- less talk about brand names, more about learning

- less money and time spent on clothes shopping, more left for educational needs

PRACTICE EXAMS

PRACTICE EXAM HEAVEN

Well, that's it! We've covered every item that the Virginia EOC English: Writing exam will test you on. To evaluate your understanding of these skills, we've written two complete practice exams based on the content that the Virginia Department of Education says it will test you on. Don't worry, you're ready. Before taking the exams, brush up on any question-type you may be rusty on, so you can get the most out of the testing material.

Each test is 44 questions long and is broken up according to the categories the Virginia Department of Education has published. For the direct-writing component of the exam, you will be provided with scratch paper and a dictionary, but not a thesaurus. During the multiple-choice component of the exam, you may not use a dictionary or a thesaurus.

Although the test will be **untimed,** you have to take it in one sitting. So to be true to the actual exam, don't break the test up into parts; take it all at once! We've provided the correct answer and a detailed explanation for every question. We want you not only to practice your test-taking skills but also to find any last-second weaknesses that you'll need to work on. It's been our pleasure to help you prepare for this exam, and we wish you the best of luck on your English: Writing EOC exam. But, of course, you won't need it.

Remember: The actual exam will have ten "field-test" questions that won't count toward your final score. Unfortunately, you won't know which are the "real" questions, so you'll have to answer them all.

···PRACTICE EXAM 1···

PRACTICE EXAM 1: ANSWER SHEET

Record your answers on this answer sheet.

1.	(A)	(B)	(C)	(D)
2.	(F)	(G)	(H)	(J)
3.	(A)	(B)	(C)	(D)
4.	(F)	(G)	(H)	(J)
5.	(A)	(B)	(C)	(D)
6.	(F)	(G)	(H)	(J)
7.	(A)	(B)	(C)	(D)
8.	(F)	(G)	(H)	(J)
9.	(A)	(B)	(C)	(D)
10.	(F)	(G)	(H)	(J)
11.	(A)	(B)	(C)	(D)
12.	(F)	(G)	(H)	(J)
13.	(A)	(B)	(C)	(D)
14.	(F)	(G)	(H)	(J)
15.	(A)	(B)	(C)	(D)
16.	(F)	(G)	(H)	(J)
17.	(A)	(B)	(C)	(D)
18.	(F)	(G)	(H)	(J)
19.	(A)	(B)	(C)	(D)
20.	(F)	(G)	(H)	(J)
21.	(A)	(B)	(C)	(D)
22.	(F)	(G)	(H)	(J)

23.	(A)	(B)	(C)	(D)
24.	(F)	(G)	(H)	(J)
25.	(A)	(B)	(C)	(D)
26.	(F)	(G)	(H)	(J)
27.	(A)	(B)	(C)	(D)
28.	(F)	(G)	(H)	(J)
29.	(A)	(B)	(C)	(D)
30.	(F)	(G)	(H)	(J)
31.	(A)	(B)	(C)	(D)
32.	(F)	(G)	(H)	(J)
33.	(A)	(B)	(C)	(D)
34.	(F)	(G)	(H)	(J)
35.	(A)	(B)	(C)	(D)
36.	(F)	(G)	(H)	(J)
37.	(A)	(B)	(C)	(D)
38.	(F)	(G)	(H)	(J)
39.	(A)	(B)	(C)	(D)
40.	(F)	(G)	(H)	(J)
41.	(A)	(B)	(C)	(D)
42.	(F)	(G)	(H)	(J)
43.	(A)	(B)	(C)	(D)
44.	(F)	(G)	(H)	(J)

Albert Einstein

Corey has been asked by his science teacher to write a short biography of Corey's favorite scientist, Albert Einstein. The biography will be displayed on a bulletin board at the school science fair.

Sample Exam Question 1

Corey made the chart below to organize the facts he has collected on his note cards. Use it to answer sample exam question 1 (SA-1).

Albert Einstein Important Facts

Childhood

1. Einstein was born in Germany in 1879, the son of a businessman specializing in electrical engineering.

2.

Young Adulthood

3. As a young man, Einstein studied electrical engineering.

4. Einstein started work at the patent office and married a Hungarian woman named Mileva.

Later Years

5. In 1922 Einstein received the Nobel Prize for physics.

6. With growing anti-Semitism in Germany, Einstein made the United States his home and became an outspoken pacifist.

SA-1 **Which of these facts should Corey put beside 2 on the chart?**

A Einstein went to the United States. mainly to raise money to build the Hebrew University in Jerusalem.

B Einstein gave his support for the Manhattan Project.

C As a schoolboy, Einstein did not do well in school and may have had a learning disability. *

D Einstein regretted signing the letter to President Roosevelt recommending the construction of atom bombs.

Go On

Here is the first part of Corey's rough draft. Use it to answer sample exam question 2 (SA-2).

(1) Albert Einstein was born in the town of Ulm in the southern part of Germany on March 14, 1879. (2) Because his father was in the electrical engineering business. (3) Albert became acquainted with the electrical industry as a young boy. (4) He did not do very well in school, though, and his headmaster predicted that he would never be successful at much of anything.

SA-2 **Which of these choices is not a complete sentence?**

F 1

G 2 *

H 3

J 4

Read this next section of Corey's rough draft and answer sample exam questions 3 and 4 (SA-3 and SA-4). This section has groups of underlined words. The questions ask about these groups of underlined words.

(5) In 1894, his father's <u>business failed, Einstein's parents moved to Italy.</u> (6) Six months later Albert quit school and joined his parents. (7) He studied at the Swiss Federal Polytechnic School in Zurich and graduated in 1900. (8) <u>He taught</u> for a while and then took a job at the Swiss Patent Office.

SA-3 **In sentence 5, how would <u>business failed, Einstein's parents moved to Italy.</u> be correctly written?**

A business failed Einstein's parents moved to Italy.

B business failed, and Einstein's parents moved to Italy. *

C business failed: Einstein's parents moved to Italy.

D As it is

SA-4 **In sentence 8, how would <u>He taught</u> be correctly written?**

F He is teaching

G He will teach

H He teach

J As it is *

1 Which of these would *best* help Stacie get started on her application essay?

A Brainstorming reasons she needs to earn some money

B Listing past jobs and experiences with music

C Writing the rough draft of her application

D Listing all the pieces she has learned to play

Here is the first part of Stacie's rough draft. Use it to answer questions 2–5.

(1) I would be a good employee at Musicland because I am responsible and hard working and love music. (2) Usually I am prompt and on time and as a rule I am very organized. (3) I am a "people-person." (4) I would interact well with customers.

(5) Currently, I perform in both the school band, where I play electric bass, and the chamber choir, where I am in the alto section. (6) I am particularly knowledgeable about contemporary music and usually choose pop for my personal listening pleasure. (7) I own all of Beck's albums and have his poster up on my wall at home. (8) In addition to popular music, I have an appreciation for jazz and classical music.

---

2 How is sentence 2 *best* rewritten?

F Usually, I am prompt, on time, and I am very organized.

G Usually I am prompt, on time, and very organized.

H Usually I am prompt and very organized.

J Usually I am very prompt, on time, and organized.

3 How can sentences 3 and 4 *best* be combined?

A I am a "people-person" who would interact well with customers.

B I am a "people-person" and interacting well with customers.

C I am a "people-person," I would interact well with customers.

D I am a "people-person," and with customers, would interact well.

4 Which sentence would be the *best* topic sentence to insert in the second paragraph before sentence 5?

  F Also, I have an in-depth knowledge of music and current musical trends.

  G I am sure that my broad knowledge about contemporary music would make me an ideal employee.

  H I am an enthusiastic musician and I am sure that this would show through in my work.

  J I am passionate about music in a variety of forms.

5 Which sentence contains information that is least relevant to Stacie's application?

  A 5

  B 6

  C 7

  D 8

Go On

Read this next section of Stacie's rough draft and answer questions 6–9. This section has groups of underlined words. The questions ask about these groups of underlined words.

(9) My math and technology skills could be put to good use as a member of your staff. (10) I am doing <u>well in Algebra II and my math</u> skills would be useful if I were working the cash register. (11) I have completed two years' worth of computer courses, including Computer Technology and Computer Applications. (12) If you need someone to take inventory on the computer or do a search for a particular CD, <u>I am more then</u> amply prepared. (13) I helped with the audio in my <u>High School production of Annie</u> last year, and would enjoy helping set up for musicians who sometimes perform at your store. (14) For the <u>past two summer's, I worked</u> at CVS Pharmacy as a cashier and left that job only because it was a temporary position. (15) I would be happy to provide the letter of recommendation written by my supervisor.

(16) In summary, I am dedicated to music and an experienced worker. (17) I like your store and want very much to work there. (18) Thank you for considering my application.

6 In sentence 10, how would <u>well in Algebra II and my math</u> be correctly written?

F good in Algebra II and my math

G well in algebra II and my math

H well in Algebra II and my Math

J As it is

7 In sentence 12, how would <u>I am more then</u> be correctly written?

A I was more then

B I am more than

C I will be more then

D As it is

8 In sentence 13, how would <u>High School production of Annie</u> be correctly written?

F high school production of *Annie*

G High School production of "Annie"

H High school production of *Annie*

J As it is

9 In sentence 14, how would <u>past two summer's, I worked</u> be correctly written?

A past two summers, I am working

B passed two summers, I worked

C past two summers, I worked

D As it is

Go On ⇒

How to Shoot a Basketball

Vaughn is working for the summer as an assistant coach at a basketball camp for middle school students. The coach plans to give campers a handout with playing tips. He asks Vaughn to write a section on how to shoot the ball properly.

Before writing his instructions, Vaughn made a list of steps he takes when using good shooting form during a game. Use it to answer question 10.

1. Start with your dominant foot forward.

2. Bend your knees.

3. Put the ball at either side of your waist.

4. Shift your weight forward to your dominant foot.

5. Step back into shooting position with the ball at your upper chest.

6. Bring the ball to your upper forehead and move it a bit to one side.

7. Bend your wrist back and make sure your dominant arm, wrist, and body make an L-shape.

8. Make sure your arms are making an up-side-down V.

9. Jump straight up and flick your wrist.

10. Release your knees before you jump, so they are straight when you spring up.

---

10 Sentence 10 is *not* in the correct sequence. Sentence 10 is *best* placed directly after —

   F sentence 4

   G sentence 6

   H sentence 7

   J sentence 8

11 Which is the *best* revision of sentence 3?

   A Right away put the ball at either side of your waist and shift your weight forward to your dominant foot.

   B Smoothly position the ball at either side of your waist and shift your weight forward to your dominant foot.

   C Make sure you have the ball at either side of your waist and shift your weight forward to your dominant foot.

   D Quickly get the ball at either side of your waist and shift your weight forward to your dominant foot.

Here is the first part of Vaughn's draft. Use it to answer questions 11–14.

(1) By following a simple set of steps, you can improve your basketball shooting. (2) Start by putting your dominant foot forward and bending your knees. (3) Have the ball at either side of your waist and shift your weight forward to your dominant foot. (4) Step backwards into a shooting position with your feet shoulder-width apart and your knees bent. (5) You want the ball to be near your upper chest area. (6) On the other hand, you do not want it too close to your body. (7) You don't want your shot to hit your chin on the way up to the basket. (8) You also don't want your shirt hanging loose or the ref might tell you to tuck it in. (9) Bring the ball to your upper forehead and move it a little bit to one side. (10) After making sure your dominant hand is on the back of the ball and your other hand is over to the side of the ball.

12 How can sentences 5 and 6 *best* be combined?

F The ball should be near your upper chest area but not too close to your body.

G You want the ball to be near your upper chest area, but not being too close to your body.

H You want the ball to be near your upper chest area, you do not want it too close to your body.

J You want the ball to be near your upper chest area, and on the other hand you do not want it too close to your body.

13 Which sentence contains information that is *least* relevant to Vaughn's instructions?

A 2

B 4

C 8

D 9

14 Which of these should be revised because it is *not* a complete sentence?

F 3

G 5

H 7

J 10

Go On

Read this next section of Vaughn's rough draft and answer questions 15–18. This section has groups of underlined words. The questions ask about these groups of underlined words.

(11) <u>Next, bend the wrist of your</u> dominant hand back. (12) You should be holding that arm up and bent at the elbow, so that it forms an L shape. (13) Both lower arms should now be raised diagonally in relation to each other <u>so that it forms</u> an upside-down V.

(14) In one continuous motion, release your knees, jump straight up, and flick the wrist of your dominant hand. (15) <u>Straighten your arm, and</u> "follow through" with your dominant hand. (16) To "follow through" properly, think of the motion involved when you put your hand into a jar and take out a pickle. (17) Make your arm go up, over, and down. (18) Finally, watch as the ball sails up, over, and through the hoop. (19) Enjoy the satisfaction of <u>knowing that youv'e made</u> a basket!

15 In sentence 11, how would <u>Next, bend the wrist of your</u> be correctly written?

A Next, bend the wrist of one's

B Next, bending the wrist of your

C Next, bend the wrist of you're

D As it is

16 In sentence 13, how would <u>so that it forms</u> be correctly written?

F so that it form

G so that they be forming

H so that they form

J As it is

17 In sentence 15, how would <u>Straighten your arm, and</u> be correctly written?

A Straighten your arm and

B straighten your arm, and

C Straiten your arm, and

D As it is

18 In sentence 19, how would <u>knowing that youv'e made</u> be correctly written?

F knowing that youve made

G knowing that you've made

H knowwing that youv'e made

J As it is

Go On

Daniella is a tenth grader entering an online writing contest sponsored by a wildlife society; winning entries will be published in a collection of animal stories. Daniella decides that her story will be about a childhood memory of one of her pets, but she hasn't selected which one, yet.

19 **Which of these would *best* help Daniella get started on her story?**

A Making up a title for her story

B Watching a public television special about unusual pets

C Listing the pets she had as a child

D Beginning to write her first draft

Here is the first part of Daniella's rough draft. Use it to answer questions 20–23.

(1) As I sit here with my old friend Felicity curled up in my lap, I remember something that happened when I was four, and I am grateful that things ended as they did. (2) It's one of my earliest memories, and I remember the whole episode in vivid detail.

(3) For my birthday on the rainy day before. (4) My parents had given me a nice, soft little kitten. (5) I had promptly named her Felicity after one of my American Girl dolls, and my new playmate quickly replaced my former favorite. (6) I had ignored my new toys and played with the furry Felicity until bedtime.

(7) I woke the next bright and sunny morning feeling elated. (8) I scooped the kitty up from my bed and skipped out to the backyard hugging her to my chest. (9) Next door a little girl with red hair was playing on our elderly neighbors' porch. (10) I recognized her vaguely because she and I had played together once or twice before when she had come to visit her grandparents. (11) When she saw me, she hopped down the stairs and ran over to see what I held.

Go On ➪

20 Which of these should be revised because it is *not* a complete sentence?

F 3

G 7

H 9

J 11

21 Which of these describes how Daniella captures the reader's attention in the introduction?

A She opens abruptly by showing the action of her story already in progress.

B She begins with an interesting piece of natural-sounding dialogue.

C She develops interest by describing a scene full of sensory detail.

D She creates suspense by raising a question in the reader's mind about what happened.

22 Which is the *best* revision of sentence 4?

F My parents had given me a very very little, two-toned kitten with great fur that was extremely soft.

G My parents had given me a wonderful, beautiful little kitten that I just loved as soon as I saw.

H My parents had given me a tiny black and white kitten with fur as soft as a caterpillar.

J My parents had given me a really great little kitten that had two colors in his fur and was so soft.

23 Which is the *best* revision of sentence 6?

A Ignoring my new toys, the furry Felicity was my playmate until bedtime.

B Ignoring my new toys, I had played with the furry Felicity until bedtime.

C I had ignored my new toys and playing with the furry Felicity until bedtime.

D I had played with the furry Felicity until bedtime and ignored my new toys.

Go On

Read this next section of Daniella's rough draft and answer questions 24–27. This section has groups of underlined words. The questions ask about these groups of underlined words.

(12) "Is that your kitty? Is it a girl or a boy?" she asked.

(13) <u>I proudly answered "Yeah, she's mine!</u> (14) I got her yesterday for my birthday and I'm naming her "Felicity."

(15) We played with her for a while by tossing a little ball for her to chase over the wet grass. (16) After a while, we tired of that and tried snaking a jump rope near her to see if we could get her to pounce. (17) We soon got bored with that, too, and looked around for some other way to <u>amuse ourself.</u> (18) Next to the back door, <u>we found a</u> large fish tank my mother had cleaned out. (19) After a day and night of heavy rain, the tank was filled to overflowing.

(20) The little red-haired girl turned to me and speculated, "I wonder if your kitty can swim. (21) Maybe we should teach her!"

(22) Reluctantly, I agreed, and we dropped poor Felicity into the tank. (23) Luckily my mother had been watching events unfold from the kitchen window. (24) She dashed outside with <u>dishtowel in hand, scoped Felicity from the water,</u> and wrapped the towel around the shivering kitten.

(25) We never did teach Felicity to swim, but I certainly learned a few lessons that day. (26) Cats and water do not mix. (27) Think twice before listening to impish red-haired girls. (28) Most important, always treat a feline friend with the same care and respect you'd show a human one. (29) Felicity quickly forgave my ignorance, thank goodness, and we have been lifelong friends ever since. (30) I never did see that red-haired girl again, though.

Go On ⇨

24 In sentence 13, how would <u>I proudly answered "Yeah, she's mine!</u> be correctly written?

   F I proudly answered, "Yeah, she's mine!

   G I answered proud "Yeah, she's mine!

   H I proudly answered "Yeah she's mine!

   J As it is

25 In sentence 17, how would <u>amuse ourself</u> be correctly written?

   A amuse myself

   B amuse herself

   C amuse ourselves

   D As it is

26 In sentence 18, how would <u>we found</u> be correctly written?

   F we are finding

   G we will find

   H we finds

   J As it is

27 In sentence 24, how would <u>dishtowel in hand, scoped Felicity from the water,</u> be correctly written?

   A dishtowel in hand scoped Felicity from the water,

   B dishtowel in hand, scooped Felicity from the water,

   C dishtowel in hand, scoped Felicity from the water

   D As it is

Go On

Cafeteria Food Consumers

Lexi has decided to write an article for her school newspaper about what three different groups of students eat in the school cafeteria.

Lexi has created a Venn diagram to start organizing her thoughts about what two groups of eaters like to buy in the school cafeteria. Use it to answer question 28.

Vegetarians	Both	Chocolate-lovers
1.	2.	3.
4.	5.	6.
7.		8.

28 **For point 2, Lexi would *most* likely choose —**

   F fast-food double cheeseburgers

   G organic tofu burgers

   H all-you-can-eat spaghetti and meatballs

   J carrot-cake fudgebars

Go On

Here is the first part of Lexi's rough draft. Use it to answer questions 29–31.

(1) Students at Roanoke Central have diverse eating habits. (2) Among the eaters with more extreme diets are the vegetarians, chocolate lovers, and being on sports teams.

(3) Vegetarians may use sound nutritional judgment in avoiding foods that raise cholesterol. (4) Complete exclusion of meat can be detrimental to health, though.

(5) Health-conscious vegetarians such as sophomore Sue Palka usually try to include as much protein in their diets as they can without eating meat. (6) Sue says she would choose a grapefruit over a candy bar any day. (7) She points out, though, that many vegetarians enjoy sweets as much as the rest of us. (8) Another common stereotype of vegetarians is that they consume only organic foods this is not always true. (9) Many vegetarians at Roanoke report that they avoid buying organic fruits and vegetables because the cost is so much higher.

29 Which of these should be revised because it is an *incorrect*, run-on sentence?

A 2

B 5

C 8

D 9

30 Which is the *best* revision of sentence 2?

F Among the eaters with more extreme diets are the vegetarians, love of chocolate, and being a sports team.

G Among the eaters with more extreme diets are the vegetarian-only, chocolate lovers, and being on a sports team.

H Among the eaters with more extreme diets are the vegetarians, chocolate lovers, and after sports practice.

J Among the eaters with more extreme diets are the vegetarians, chocolate lovers, and members of sports teams.

31 How can sentences 3 and 4 *best* be combined?

A Using sound nutritional judgment in avoiding foods that raise cholesterol, complete exclusion of meat can be detrimental to vegetarians' health.

B Although vegetarians may use sound nutritional judgment in avoiding foods that raise cholesterol, complete exclusion of meat can be detrimental to health.

C Avoiding foods that raise cholesterol, sound nutritional judgment in complete exclusion of meat can be detrimental to health.

D Raising cholesterol, meat should be completely excluded but sound nutritional judgment used to avoid detriment to health.

Go On

Read this next section of Lexi's rough draft and answer questions 32–35. This section has groups of underlined words. The questions ask about these groups of underlined words.

(10) <u>Those who crave chocolate comprise</u> a far-ranging group of eaters that includes vegetarians and omnivores, alike. (11) However, chocoholics <u>hardly never eat much fruit</u> or meat or anything from any of the basic food groups, for that matter. (12) Justin Ward, a senior, is a classic example of the true chocoholic. (13) <u>Spotted laying on the school's front lawn</u> with a Snickers bar in hand, Justin admitted that his appetite for vegetables is minimal. (14) "I wouldn't be caught dead with a celery stick in my hand unless it were <u>covered with chocolate" he swore.</u>

(15) Athletes often change their eating habits during their sports seasons. (16) The same students who try to watch their waistlines during the off-season can be found wolfing down spaghetti at pasta parties before track and swim meets. (17) On the other hand, guys who don't ordinarily count calories seem to have more prominent cheekbones and baggier clothing during the winter wrestling season. (18) Taking extreme measures to keep their weight within a predetermined range can even result in alarming eating disorders among these athletes.

(19) Cartoons and the popular press typically portray students eating fast-food burgers and fries. (20) In actuality, if students at Central are any reflection of teenage society as a whole, teens have multifarious eating habits.

Go On

32 In sentence 10, how would <u>Those who crave chocolate comprise</u> be correctly written?

    F Those who craves chocolate comprise

    G Those who crave chocolate comprises

    H Those whom crave chocolate comprise

    J As it is

33 In sentence 11, how would <u>hardly never eat much fruit</u> be correctly written?

    A hardly never ate much fruit

    B hardly ever eat much fruit

    C hardly never will eat much fruit

    D As it is

34 In sentence 13, how would <u>Spotted laying on the school's front lawn</u> be correctly written?

    F Spotted lying on the school's front lawn

    G Spoted laying on the school's front lawn

    H Spotted laying on the schools front lawn

    J As it is

35 In sentence 14, how would <u>covered with chocolate" he swore</u> be correctly written?

    A covered with chocolate," he sweared.

    B covered with chocolate!," he swore.

    C covered with chocolate!" he swore.

    D As it is

Go On ⇨

School Uniforms

Christine and Elijah want to write editorials for their school newspaper about a recent proposal to require school uniforms. Elijah is in favor of the idea, but Christine is against it.

Elijah has created a basic outline to organize his thoughts. Use it to answer question 36.

    I. Clothing and crime

    II. Segregation of different groups

    III. Distraction from learning

36 **Under heading III, Elijah is *most* likely to add —**

  F Uniforms would help break down divisions between student groups

  G There would be more focus on schoolwork and less on looking good

  H Uniforms would cut down on gang violence

  J Fewer clothing items would be stolen

Go On

Draft A below is Elijah's rough draft of the first part of his article. Draft B is Christine's rough draft. Use both drafts to answer questions 37–40.

DRAFT A: Elijah's Draft

Several public schools across the nation now require their students to wear uniforms. I am in favor of instituting a uniform policy in our state's schools. Other states that have adopted such a policy report less violent behavior and crime, better relations among students, and an improved learning environment.

Uniforms would cut down on crime. For example, Chicago schools reported a decline in gang violence. After uniforms became mandatory. Trouble is less likely to start when gang emblems and colors are not being paraded through the halls. A policy of uniforms also cuts down on general theft. The reason for this is that clothing items are less prone to disappearing when everyone has the same outfit. Who needs another shirt just like the one you already have?

DRAFT B: Christine's Draft

Uniforms are the last thing we need. We have a hard enough time already. It's already hard enough expressing ourselves. Why should we be forced in one more way to act like robots? Parents and students and maybe our principal should decide. The state shouldn't be the one deciding on our dress code.

People who support uniforms say it would reduce violence and crime in schools. Instead of telling students what they have to wear, let's come up with some real solutions to the problem of violence and things being stolen. The real answer would be to put in metal detectors and hiring more security. These would reduce guns and other weapons in school. Perhaps police officers that are off-duty could be hired as guards for security. They could also help teach the program against drugs and that way the school could save money they would have spent on paying for more teachers to teach that program.

Go On ➡

37 Which paragraph gives better reasons for the author's position?

   A Paragraph 1 of Draft A, because it asks a thought-provoking question

   B Paragraph 1 of Draft A, because it mentions the results of the policy in other states

   C Paragraph 1 of Draft B, because it mentions how hard it is for students to express themselves

   D Paragraph 1 of Draft B, because it says parents and students should decide

38 The first sentence of Draft A is more effective than the first sentence of Draft B because it —

   F makes a direct, persuasive appeal to the reader

   G introduces the topic with relevant background information

   H adopts a bitter, angry tone

   J uses more descriptive language

39 What is the main difference between paragraph 2 of Draft A and paragraph 2 of Draft B?

   A All the sentences in paragraph 2 of Draft B support the topic sentence.

   B The sentences in paragraph 2 of Draft A support the central idea with specific examples and explanations.

   C The sentences in paragraph 2 of Draft B all contain information that is relevant to the writer's argument.

   D The sentences in paragraph 2 of Draft A have all been revised to eliminate fragments.

40 <u>Perhaps police officers that are off-duty could be hired as guards for security.</u> In paragraph 2 of Draft B, which of these is a problem with the sentence?

   A It should be moved to the beginning of the paragraph.

   B It expresses Christine's personal opinion about school security.

   C It uses too many words and could be made simpler.

   D It contradicts the rest of Christine's argument.

Read this next section of Christine's rough draft and answer questions 41–44. This section has groups of underlined words. The questions ask about these groups of underlined words.

Money is <u>an issue since uniforms</u> are rather expensive. I would not want to spend money on costly uniforms. I would rather pay <u>for clothes I can wear to school work, the mall,</u> and other places. All-purpose clothing is economical. <u>Who wants to buy seperate outfits?</u>

Self-expression is even more of an issue. In other <u>countries, such as china, school</u> uniforms are required in public as well as private schools. I am happy that we don't yet have the same custom in all U.S. schools. Every teen has the desire to express himself or herself and one way is by wearing clothes that state, "This is me." A uniform policy would take away from our sense of style and more importantly it would detract from our sense of self.

41 How would <u>an issue since uniforms</u> be correctly written?

   A an issue. Since uniforms

   B a issue since uniforms

   C an issue sense uniforms

   D As it is

42 How would <u>clothes I can wear to school work, the mall,</u> be correctly written —

   F clothes I can wear to school, work, the mall,

   G cloths I can wear to school work, the mall,

   H clothes I can wear to school work, going to the mall,

   J As it is

43 How would <u>Who wants to buy seperate outfits?</u> be correctly written?

   A Who wants to by seperate outfits?

   B Who wants to buy separate outfits?

   C Who wants to buy separate outfits.

   D As it is

44 How would <u>countries, such as china, school</u> be correctly written?

   F countrys, such as china, school

   G countries such as china school

   H countries, such as China, school

   J As it is

Go On

WRITING PROMPT

> **What do you think is the best (or worst) advice you ever received? Why was it the best (or worst)? Be sure to explain and support your answer with reasons and examples.**

Writing Checklist

___ Did I plan and organize the paper before writing it?

Did I revise the paper to include

    ___ an attention-getting introduction?

    ___ plenty of specific, supporting evidence for the central idea?

    ___ only ideas that support that main idea?

    ___ sentences and paragraphs that follow a logical order?

    ___ sentences that are clear, varied, and smooth flowing?

    ___ vocabulary that conveys a tone appropriate for my audience and purpose?

    ___ a conclusion that offers a wrap-up without just saying the same thing again?

Did I edit the paper to make sure that

    ___ grammar is correct?

    ___ capitalization is correct?

    ___ fragments and run-ons are eliminated?

    ___ misplaced modifiers are put in the right place?

    ___ spelling is error-free?

Did I go over the paper to ensure that

    ___ my purpose in writing the paper is clearly communicated?

    ___ the paper accomplishes what it is supposed to?

Go On ⇨

Go On

Go On

ANSWERS AND EXPLANATIONS
FOR PRACTICE EXAM 1

ANSWERS AND EXPLANATIONS FOR PRACTICE EXAM 1

ANSWER KEY

MULTIPLE CHOICE

1 **B** Stacie needs to come up with as many reasons as she can why the store should hire her. Her potential employer is mainly interested in her past jobs and relevant experience (**B**)—*not* why she needs money (**A**) or the exact pieces she can play (**D**). Reject **C** because if she starts right in on the rough draft without doing any prewriting/planning first, she may find she doesn't know what to say.

2 **H** *Remember*: Keep it short and simple. Because "prompt" means "on time," you don't need to say both.

3 **A** You could use Backsolving here: Without even looking at the original essay, you could use POE to get rid of **B**, **C**, and **D** because all three have errors in sentence formation. **B** isn't parallel ("I *am*...and *interacting...*"). **C** contains a comma-splice error because the two ideas incorrectly joined by the comma are each complete by themselves (see page 100) — "I am..." contains a subject and verb and so does "I would interact...." **D** sounds awkward, with words out of order ("with customers, would interact well"). Choice **A** is the only one that is error-free and has a nice, smooth rhythm.

4 **J** What is the topic of the second paragraph? The paragraph is about Stacie's passion for music—playing it and listening to it. The main idea that the sentences in this paragraph support is that Stacie is passionate about music in a variety of forms. She then goes on to describe these forms: playing electric bass, singing, and listening to a variety of types of music. The topic sentence has to be like an umbrella—something that will cover all the other sentences. For this reason, you can reject **F** and **G** as too narrow in one direction (they refer to her knowledge, but not her performance) and **H** as too narrow in the other (it refers to her playing, but not her knowledge).

5 **C** Stacie needs to keep her purpose and audience in mind from beginning to end. What is she trying to do? She is doing all she can to convince the hirers at Musicland that she would make a good employee. Will they care that she has Beck's poster on her wall? Probably not. On the other hand, they will be interested in her experience with and knowledge of music (**A**, **B**, and **D**), since customers will appreciate getting help from someone who "knows her stuff."

6   J   Capitalize names of particular courses (Algebra II), but not general subjects (math).

7   B   Don't get tripped up by frequently confused words like then/than and accept/except. Use "than" for comparison and "then" for time. You had more *than* I. You ate yours and *then* I ate mine.

8   F   Capitalize "high school" only when it is contained in the name of a particular school: The high school I graduated from was called Fred Farkle High School.

9   C   Don't overuse apostrophes. You often need them to show possession (Henry's poptart) or in contractions (He's happy), but never for plain old plurals (two summers). Once you spot the apostrophe error in the underlined section, you can guess aggressively that your answer will be the one that corrects it—"past two summers, I worked"—and zero in on **C**. Even if you don't see the error in the original sentence right away, you can eliminate choices **A** and **B** because each introduces a new error. **A** has a tense error (the words "past two summers" clue you in to the fact that you need a past-tense verb— "**worked**"). **B** uses the wrong word of a pair that is frequently confused: passed (verb)/past (adjective).

10   J   You don't have to know anything about basketball to answer this question. You just need to remember one pretty obvious thing: When you're giving step-by-step directions, it makes sense to mention steps in the order they're taken. Vaughn mixes up two steps (9 and 10) when he describes how to jump, then mentions what you do "before you jump."

11   B   The EOC-scorers want to see that you know how to choose words carefully. While verbs like "have," "put," and "get" are vague, the phrase "smoothly position" tells precisely what action should be taken.

12   F   Look for the combination that is smooth, meaningful, concise, and error-free. **G** is awkward and has an error in parallelism ("to be *near*, but not *being too close*..."). **H** is a comma splice because a comma incorrectly connects two complete ideas that could each stand alone as a sentence. **J** isn't as concise as **F**. Remember to trim the fat: Why use "and on the other hand" when you could just use "but" and why repeat "want"? ("You want...you do not want...")

13   C   Vaughn's purpose is to teach the campers how to shoot the ball. He loses sight of that purpose for a moment when he goes off on a tangent about what the referee might say about shirts that aren't tucked in.

14   J   Remember to be suspicious of *-ing* words like "making." Always check that you have a complete idea, with a subject and verb. The fragment in sentence 10 leaves you hanging, wondering, "Who does what after making sure all of this stuff about where your two hands go?"

15 **D** There's nothing wrong here. Eliminate **A**. Vaughn has been using the pronouns "you" and "your" throughout the article, so he shouldn't switch to "one." Scratch **B**. It creates a fragment with no verb, since "bending" is a noun. Get rid of **C** because it incorrectly substitutes "you're" (the contraction of "you are") for the correct possessive, "your."

16 **H** Remember whenever you see a pronoun like "*it*," to check agreement. The pronoun, here, replaces "both lower arms" and should be "they." The pronoun "*it*" does not agree with this antecedent. You could zap **F** and **G** by POE, anyway, since both contain errors. The subject and verb don't agree in **F** ("it forms," not "it form"). Standard, correct written usage is "they are forming"—not "they be forming": **G**.

17 **A** Don't overuse commas. "Straighten your arm" and "follow through" are simply a pair of actions. You only need a comma before "and" if you have a list of three or more items (like "Straighten your arm, follow through, and meditate on your belly button") or if the word *and* separates two complete ideas, each with a subject and verb (such as "Jerrold straightens out his arm from shoulder to wrist, and Tamara follows through on her serve").

18 **G** When forming contractions, be careful to place the apostrophe (') where the missing letter(s) would have gone. The contraction for "you have" is "you've." The apostrophe fits right where the *ha* in "have" used to be.

19 **C** It's often better to wait until you've completed at least a rough draft before choosing a title, since your main idea often shifts during the planning stages, so cross off **A**. You often need a jump-start such as brainstorming to get the ideas flowing before you can begin your draft, so eliminate **D**. Watching the special would probably give you plenty of ideas—but not ideas you could use in a story about your own pet—so forget **B**. By first listing all the pets she had as a child, Daniella can narrow down her topic to one particular pet.

20 **F** Choice **F** is a fragment. The idea in line 3 is incomplete because it lacks both subject and verb. Who did what (for my birthday)?

21 **D** All of these describe ways Daniella might have hooked her reader in the opener, but only **D** describes what she actually did. She made the reader want to read on and find out the answer to this question: What happened when Daniella was four and why is she grateful about the way things turned out?

22 **H** Eliminate choices **F**, **G**, and **J** because they contain words that are just as anemic, overused, and vague as those in the original. Usually try to avoid descriptions like "great," "wonderful," "beautiful," and "so soft." Notice that choice **C**, with the vivid comparison "soft as a caterpillar"—helps you *see* and *feel* this kitten in your mind's eye more precisely than the other, often longer, descriptions.

23 **B** Time to apply POE! Eliminate **A** because it contains a misplaced modifier. The descriptive phrase "ignoring my new toys" isn't next to the person it modifies, "*I*." Instead, it sounds like Felicity is the one ignoring the toys! Get rid of **C** because there is a problem with parallelism: "I had ignored...and playing..." Although there isn't anything wrong with **D**, it does not correct the original problem—lack of variety. Sentences 4, 5, and 6 all begin the same way: *Somebody had* done this, *somebody had* done that, *somebody had* done another thing. Choice **B** lends more sentence variety by beginning with an introductory phrase, "Ignoring my new toys."

24 **F** Only choice **F** supplies the comma that is necessary to separate the words in quotations from the words that tell who said them.

25 **C** Eliminate choice **D**, "as it is," right off the bat because there is no such word as "ourself"! You need to replace it with the pronoun that agrees with "we": "ourselves."

26 **J** The verb tense is fine as it is—past tense—since that is consistent with the tense of other verbs in this story about the past. That lets off **F** (present tense) and **G** (future tense). Eliminate **H**, "we finds," because the subject and verb do not agree. The plural subject, *we*, requires a plural verb, *find*: *we find*.

27 **B** You don't even need to look back at the original story. Doesn't one misspelled word—"scoped"— leap out at you when you run your eyes over the question? Remember the consonant-doubling rule that applies to one-syllable words: scoop/scooped, shop/shopped, slap/slapped.

28 **J** Point 2 is in the circled area of the diagram shared by both groups of eaters. That means it is a type of food enjoyed by both types. By POE, cross off **F** because vegetarians don't eat cheeseburgers and chocolate lovers may or may not eat them. Eliminate **G** because chocolate lovers may or may not like tofu. Get rid of **H** because vegetarians don't eat meatballs. That leaves **J**. Since the bars contain both vegetables (carrots) and chocolate (fudge), they should appeal to both vegetarians and chocolate lovers.

29 **C** This is actually two complete ideas, incorrectly fused. The first part, "Another common stereotype of vegetarians is that they consume only organic foods," is a complete idea, with a subject (*stereotype*) and a verb (*is*), that could stand on its own. The second part, "this is not always true," is also a complete idea (subject—*this*, verb—*is*) that could stand alone.

30 J Sentence 2 has a problem with parallelism that needs correction. Since Lexi is describing three similar groups (all are groups of eaters), she needs to use a similar form to describe all three. "Vegetarians" and "chocolate lovers" are both people, but "being on sports teams" is an action. The people on those teams might be described as "members of sports teams." Choice **F** makes the problem with parallelism worse: now you have a group of people (*vegetarians*) listed with two actions (*love...and being...*). Choice **G** is no better, since it contains a diet (*vegetarian-only*), a group (*chocolate lovers*), and an action (*being on a sports team*). Choice **H** is wrong, too, since it contains two groups (*vegetarians* and *chocolate lovers*), with a time thrown in (*after sports practice*).

31 B Sentences 3 and 4 contain contrasting ideas. The smoothest way to combine such choppy, contrasting ideas is often by connecting them with words such as "but" or "while." Choices **A** and **C** are wrong because they add a new problem—a misplaced modifier.

In choice **A**, because "complete exclusion" comes right after the describing phrase "Using sound nutritional judgment," it wrongly sounds as if exclusion of meat is using judgment! Likewise, choice **C** sounds as if sound judgment is avoiding foods. It's the vegetarians who are excluding meat and using sound judgment!

Choice **D** doesn't work because it not only sounds awkward, but changes the meaning of the original. Lexi doesn't mean to say that it is necessary to exclude meat from a healthy diet. She wants to stress that while such a decision may be sound, it may also cause health problems if good judgment isn't used.

32 J The EOC exam-makers want you to know pronoun case (Do I use *I* or *me*? *We* or *us*? *Who* or *whom*?) I wonder *who* gave the most trouble *to whom*? (In Lexi's draft, *who*—the subject of *crave*—is used correctly.) They also want you to know how to make subjects and verbs agree. Here, you use Thelma's Rule of Thumb to make sure that the plural subject (*Those*) has a plural verb (*comprise*).

33 B Beware double negatives! Since "hardly" already contains "not" in its meaning (not often or not much) you don't need another negative word ("never").
Incorrect: They hardly never eat much fruit.
Correct: They hardly ever eat much fruit. They almost never eat fruit.

34 **F** The Virginia Department of Education specifically mentions the common usage problem lie/lay on a list of errors that could be tested on the EOC Exam. Learn when to use which one now, once and for all! (See page 79.) He was *lying* on the front lawn. He was *laying* his blanket on the front lawn. Only choice **F** corrects the shameful misuse of "laying" in the original sentence. Besides, there is a misspelling in **G** ("Spoted"), and the apostrophe is missing from the possessive in **H** ("schools").

35 **C** *Remember: Usually* when you write out dialogue, you need a comma to separate the speaker from the words in quotes (see page 99)—whether the speaker is mentioned first (He says, "Blah-de-blah") or second ("Blah-de-blah," he says.) *However*, if there's an exclamation point at the end of the quoted words, it's exception time and you *don't* need a comma. Get rid of **B**, then, because the comma is unnecessary. Eliminate **A** because the past tense of the irregular verb, "swear," is "swore," just as the past tense of "wear" is "wore."

36 **G** Under heading III, *Distraction from learning*, should go any related ideas. In other words, how would uniforms help students concentrate on learning? **G** fits here, perfectly: students would pay less attention to looking good and more attention to schoolwork. **F** belongs under heading II and **H** and **J** belong under heading I in the outline.

37 **B** Questions like this one require you to step back from both articles so that you can compare them. First get the gist of what each is saying and form a general opinion of how well the writer succeeded. It's clear that Elijah is for uniforms while Christine is against them. You may also notice that Elijah's draft is better written than Christine's. His first paragraph clearly defines his position and outlines the organization his argument will follow. Hers is a set of vague, angry, disconnected statements ("Uniforms are the last thing we need...Parents and students...should decide. The state shouldn't be the one deciding...") His sentences are smooth and varied; hers are choppy and repetitive. You can eliminate **C** and **D** because both focus on Christine's opinions instead of the reasons for her opinions. How hard it is for students to express themselves and who should decide are matters of opinion, not reasons.

38 **G** You are looking for how Elijah's first sentence is better than Christine's. Eliminate **F** and **H** because Elijah's first sentence doesn't try to persuade and certainly isn't angry. It also isn't very descriptive (**J**). But it does introduce the topic with relevant background about public schools requiring uniforms, whereas Christine's first sentence offers her opinion without any context.

39 **B** Again, you are looking for a way that Elijah's and Christine's writing is not alike. Choices **A** and **C** won't work because it is Draft A, not Draft B, that contains specific examples (Elijah cites a specific decline in violence noted in Chicago to support his argument, for example) and eliminates irrelevant ones (as when Christine tosses in the idea of police officers as drug-awareness instructors, out of nowhere). Choice **D** should be crossed off because there actually is a fragment in Elijah's draft ("After uniforms became mandatory.").

40 **C** Choices **A** and **D** say the sentence doesn't relate well to other parts of the essay. Check first to see if the problem is in the sentence itself. "Police officers that are off-duty" and "guards for security" are needlessly wordy. Eliminate **B** because you would expect Christine to express a personal opinion here.

41 **D** Spelling and usage are fine as-is in this one. Look carefully and you will see that each of the other choices adds an error: **A** creates a fragment ("Since uniforms are rather expensive"). **B** replaces the correct "an issue" with "a issue." (*Remember:* By convention we use "an" before a word beginning with a vowel.) **C** contains a misspelling of since ("sense").

42 **F** Separate three or more items in a series with commas (see page 96). Using POE, you can quickly cross **G** and **H** off your list. **G** contains a common misspelling ("cloths" instead of "clothes") and **H** contains the comma error in the original plus a new error in parallelism. (*School* and *work* are parallel to each other, but they don't line up with *going* to the mall, do they? Express similar ideas in similar form: "school, work, the mall.")

43 **B** The word *separate* is one of those commonly used and commonly misspelled words you have to drill into your brain: s-e-p-A-r-a-t-e (see page 85 for commonly misspelled words). Of course you wouldn't have fallen for choice **C**, would you? End a question with a question mark.

44 **H** Capitalize proper nouns (such as the names of countries like China), as well as proper adjectives morphed from those proper nouns (like Chinese food). Forget **F** because "countrys" is misspelled. With any word that ends consonant + *y*, change *y* to *i* before adding *s*: country becomes countries (see page 86). Forget **G** because it is missing two things: a capital letter (China) and a comma after the introductory phrase that leads up to the subject, "school uniforms."

ESSAY

What do you think is the best (or worst) advice you ever received? Why was it the best (or worst)? Be sure to explain and support your answer with reasons and examples.

Sample Essay A: A Superior Essay

Each fictional scorer gave the essay a top score of 12 for a total of 24 points.

The best piece of advice I ever recieved was from my grandmother, who lived with us until she died a year ago. Omah always loved to remind me to "stop and smell the flowers." What she meant was that it is important, no matter how hectic things are, to take the time to appreciate the small things that surround you. She believed that doing so improves your physical and mental health and also makes life better for the people around you. I didn't really pay much attention to what she believed until she was gone and, in fact, often actively resisted doing anything she suggested. It is only recently that I've come to realize how right she was and tried to follow her advice.

Omah long knew what health researchers have recently discovered. Rushing through life leads to stress, and stress can lead to a variety of health problems. Just a few of these include: headaches, ulcers, high blood pressure, and weight problems. Taking time to enjoy the little things on the other hand leads to improved health. It makes sense when you think about it, and it has been confirmed by scientific studies. Every time I take a stroll in the fresh air instead of gulping down a soda and a doughnut to wake myself up, the way I used to, I know I am doing my body a favor. Whenever I take a few minutes out to pet my cat and enjoy her purring, instead of growing annoyed with her for walking on the keyboard, I'm probably keeping my blood pressure down. And now that I take a second to look out the window each morning and enjoy the sunrise, I'm probably less of a candidate for an ulcer than I was when I'd roll out of bed and dash to catch the schoolbus or find a parking place in the overcrowded lot.

Omah firmly believed that setting aside time for quiet contemplation is important to mental health, too. Before I decided to heed my grandmother's advice, I was a nervous wreck much of the time. I found that I was often saying to myself, "just get through this."

The problem with that attitude is that you can end up living from self-imposed crisis to crisis. You start to feel that there is no "light at the end of the tunnel" and that tomorrow there is just as much to get through as today. One day I decided to slow down and start living more for the moment, as my grandmother was suggesting. I got some self-help books out of the library on relaxation techniques. I set aside some time each day for pleasurable activities like having picnics in the park with friends in the spring or shuffling through the leaves in the fall. Soon I found that I was feeling happier. I felt less overwhelmed and stressed. And as I relaxed, I felt better about myself.

Finally, Omah maintained that "taking time to smell the flowers" makes a person nicer to be around. I have seen over and over how Type-A behavior can stress out everyone around you. The person who cuts you off in traffic or shoves you in the hallway or pushes ahead of you in line sends the unpleasant message that his time is more important than yours. Rather than barging through in these situations, I find it much more pleasant to show a little courtesy, listen to a little music, or enjoy a little people-watching, and I hope that by doing so I am making life a little easier for everyone in the crowd.

The person who is always complaining about how much he has to do makes it hard for anyone else to relax. The day I decided to stop complaining and procrastinating, I know I became easier to live with. Now instead of grumbling about all I have to do, I try to spend that time doing it—and whenever possible, enjoying it. As a result, I have more time for my friends and I spend that time having fun with them instead of always using them as sounding boards.

My grandmother was a fountain of wisdom, but she wasn't always right. She advised that it was best to "starve a cold and feed a fever," but there probably is not much scientific evidence to support that idea. She also suggested that "you should try everything at least once," and I have definitely discovered that there are some things you probably should not try. When it comes to her ideas on flower-smelling, though, I think she hit the nail on the head.

Composing Domain: 4

Written Expression Domain: 4

Sentence Formation/Usage/Mechanics Domain: 4

This paper receives a score of 4 for the composing and written expression domains. This writer states her main idea (that her grandmother's advice to "stop and smell the flowers" was good counsel) clearly and keeps her essay sharply focused throughout. She employs the introduction, body, and conclusion format to make her essay easy to follow. She clarifies what her grandmother meant and supplies several illustrations, examples, reasons, and events in support—some from current health research, others anecdotal. Throughout the composition, she makes effective use of transitional phrases that make her organizational structure clear (e.g., *until*, *recently*, *on the other hand*, *whenever*, etc.). The word choice is excellent, sentence structure is varied, and voice is distinctive, making this essay interesting to read. The essay begins with a strong lead and a sophisticated, humorous close rounds out what is a superior attempt at meeting the requirements of the writing task.

The paper also merits a 4 in the usage/mechanics domain even though the writer misspells "recieved" in the first line and omits commas around an interrupter ("on the other hand"). Despite these errors, her sentence formation is appropriately mature and all of the other usage and mechanical features are correct.

Sample Essay B: A Minimally Passing Essay

Each fictional scorer gave the essay a score of 5 for a total of 10 points.

The worst advice I ever got was the old expression that "no pain equals no gain." This is bad advice when you exersize and having to do with relationships or life. When you work-out its true you usally do have to have a little bit of discomfort to see good results, major pain can mean an injury. Pain usually does'nt equal gain in life. If I fall and skin my knee I have gained nothing. Pain or discomfort in relationships usally means that something has gone bad. And little if any thing good can come out of it. Pain usally comes in school from when one isnt doing what you're supposed to. Youve either been slacking off or doing something that they want to do instead of supposed to do. The pain you're haveing is not good. Oftentimes one can gain with no pain at all on the other hand. For example I resently won a great door prize at a dance. I had no cost to myself for this gain. If you get praise for a good paper or performance thats gain without any pain on your part. In dietting oftentimes pain can lead to exactly the oposite. New fad diets call for rapid wieght loss and in the prosess proteen is burnt. Your hard work is actally hurting you in this case. One example of no pain no gain in exesize is when I was on the track and my coaches favorite motto is No Pain No Gain. I had an awful bad pain in my knee but kept runing anyway. Him and me didn't see eye to eye on if I should stop so thats why. It turned out I had a bad torn aligment and I made it worser by exersizing on it. In this case no pain no gain sure did not hold true. When my dog died last year. I went through a lot of pain. I didnt realize till she was gone how much she ment to me. It's true that you don't really apreshiate how great something is till you don't have it any more. In summary, its far from true that no pain no gain in exersize, relationships, and life.

Composing Domain: 2

Written Expression Domain: 2

Sentence Formation/Usage/Mechanics Domain: 1

For the composing and written expression domains, this paper scores a 2. No central idea is consistently present; several ideas compete. Only a few brief details are offered for elaboration. This is more a list of general statements than an organized essay. Vocabulary is repetitious and bland. (Anemic words like "good," bad," "great" are pervasive, sentence beginnings are not very varied, and voice is barely discernible.) The opening and closing are present, but underdeveloped, with few transitions to connect ideas. There are point-of-view shifts and significant digressions—particularly at the end, where the writer goes off on a tangent (about losing her dog) that does not support her main idea.

The piece is a 1 in the usage/mechanics domain because there is almost no control. There are usage errors (e.g., "made it worser") and serious spelling errors. Misspelled words are common and many of the words are ones that eleventh graders should know (e.g., actually, weight, meant). Such spelling errors distract from the message of the essay. There are also: a glaring pronoun case error ("Him and me"), comma splices (third sentence), fragments (e.g., "When my dog died last year."), several apostrophe omissions, and a nearly complete absence of commas where they're needed. The formatting convention of paragraph indentation has been ignored.

PRACTICE EXAM 2

PRACTICE EXAM 2: ANSWER SHEET

Record your answers on this answer sheet.

1. (A) (B) (C) (D)   23. (A) (B) (C) (D)
2. (F) (G) (H) (J)   24. (F) (G) (H) (J)
3. (A) (B) (C) (D)   25. (A) (B) (C) (D)
4. (F) (G) (H) (J)   26. (F) (G) (H) (J)
5. (A) (B) (C) (D)   27. (A) (B) (C) (D)
6. (F) (G) (H) (J)   28. (F) (G) (H) (J)
7. (A) (B) (C) (D)   29. (A) (B) (C) (D)
8. (F) (G) (H) (J)   30. (F) (G) (H) (J)
9. (A) (B) (C) (D)   31. (A) (B) (C) (D)
10. (F) (G) (H) (J)   32. (F) (G) (H) (J)
11. (A) (B) (C) (D)   33. (A) (B) (C) (D)
12. (F) (G) (H) (J)   34. (F) (G) (H) (J)
13. (A) (B) (C) (D)   35. (A) (B) (C) (D)
14. (F) (G) (H) (J)   36. (F) (G) (H) (J)
15. (A) (B) (C) (D)   37. (A) (B) (C) (D)
16. (F) (G) (H) (J)   38. (F) (G) (H) (J)
17. (A) (B) (C) (D)   39. (A) (B) (C) (D)
18. (F) (G) (H) (J)   40. (F) (G) (H) (J)
19. (A) (B) (C) (D)   41. (A) (B) (C) (D)
20. (F) (G) (H) (J)   42. (F) (G) (H) (J)
21. (A) (B) (C) (D)   43. (A) (B) (C) (D)
22. (F) (G) (H) (J)   44. (F) (G) (H) (J)

Albert Einstein

Corey has been asked by his science teacher to write a short biography of Corey's favorite scientist, Albert Einstein. The biography will be displayed on a bulletin board at the school science fair.

Sample Exam Question 1

Corey made the chart below to organize the facts he has collected on his note cards. Use it to answer sample exam question 1 (SA-1).

Albert Einstein Important Facts

Childhood

1. Einstein was born in Germany in 1879, the son of a businessman specializing in electrical engineering.

2.

Young Adulthood

3. As a young man, Einstein studied electrical engineering.

4. Einstein started work at the patent office and married a Hungarian woman named Mileva.

Later Years

5. In 1922, Einstein received the Nobel Prize for physics.

6. With growing anti-Semitism in Germany, Einstein made the United States his home and became an outspoken pacifist.

SA-1 **Which of these facts should Corey put beside 2 on the chart?**

A Einstein went to the United States mainly to raise money to build the Hebrew University in Jerusalem.

B Einstein gave his support for the Manhattan Project.

C As a schoolboy, Einstein did not do well in school and may have had a learning disability. *

D Einstein regretted signing the letter to President Roosevelt recommending the construction of atom bombs.

Go On ⟩

Here is the first part of Corey's rough draft. Use it to answer sample exam question 2 (SA-2).

(1) Albert Einstein was born in the town of Ulm in the southern part of Germany on March 14, 1879. (2) Because his father was in the electrical engineering business. (3) Albert became acquainted with the electrical industry as a young boy. (4) He did not do very well in school, though, and his headmaster predicted that he would never be successful at much of anything.

SA-2 Which of these choices is *not* a complete sentence?

F 1

G 2 *

H 3

J 4

Read this next section of Corey's rough draft and answer sample exam questions 3 and 4 (SA-3 and SA-4). This section has groups of underlined words. The questions ask about these groups of underlined words.

(5) In 1894, his father's <u>business failed, Einstein's parents moved to Italy.</u> (6) Six months later Albert quit school and joined his parents. (7) He studied at the Swiss Federal Polytechnic School in Zurich and graduated in 1900. (8) <u>He taught</u> for a while and then took a job at the Swiss Patent Office.

SA-3 In sentence 5, how would <u>business failed, Einstein's parents moved to Italy.</u> be correctly written?

A business failed Einstein's parents moved to Italy.

B business failed, and Einstein's parents moved to Italy. *

C business failed: Einstein's parents moved to Italy.

D As it is

SA-4 In sentence 8, how would <u>He taught</u> be correctly written?

F He is teaching

G He will teach

H He teach

J As it is *

Preventing Procrastination

Fiona is the advice columnist for the school newspaper. She receives a letter from someone who has a problem putting homework off until the last minute.

Before writing her letter in response, Fiona made a list of steps to take in order to avoid procrastination.

1. Buy a weekly assignment book with blocks for each day of the week.
2. Immediately write down daily assignments in your book.
3. For long-term projects, note on the deadline date that the project is due.
4. List the small steps that are involved in the project.
5. Jot reminders to complete these small steps on several days before the final deadline.

1 Which of these strategies would be the *most* helpful?

A As you finish each daily assignment, check it off in your assignment book.

B Sit down in the same place at the same time each day to work on daily assignments.

C Ask yourself why you tend to put schoolwork off and what you can do about it.

D Think about ways to make each homework assignment more fun.

Here is the first part of Fiona's rough draft. Use it to answer questions 2–5.

Dear Procrastinator,

(1) I'm sure that your letter rang a bell with many readers. (2) It's not uncommon to put off daunting or unpleasant tasks. (3) When procrastination becomes a routine and causes your grades to suffer, though, you have a problem. (4) I'm glad that you wrote to me because I have some advice that I think will help.

(5) There are some simple steps you can take, these steps will help you manage your time for doing homework. (6) First, get a weekly assignment book. (7) I recommend getting a large one that has blocks for each day of the week. (8) When your teacher gives daily assignments. (9) Write them down immediately in the book. (10) That way you won't forget later what you're supposed to do.

---

2 In writing paragraph 1, Fiona *most* likely tried to —

F state her ideas in a way that would grab the reader's attention

G reassure the reader by adopting an understanding tone

H criticize the reader for treating her homework so irresponsibly

J clearly and simply explain how to avoid procrastination

3 Which of these choices should be revised because it is *not* a complete sentence?

A 1

B 3

C 7

D 8

4 Which of these sentences should be revised because it is a run-on sentence?

F 3

G 4

H 5

J 6

5 Which is the *best* revision of sentence 6?

A First, invest in a weekly assignment book.

B First, get yourself a weekly assignment book.

C First, consider getting yourself a weekly assignment book.

D First, take out a weekly assignment book.

Go On →

Read this next section of Fiona's rough draft and answer questions 33–36. This section has groups of underlined words. The questions ask about these groups of underlined words.

(12) As soon as you learn when a long-term project is <u>due, flip to the deadline date in you're</u> assignment book. (13) Mark in red ink that the project is due on that day. (14) Then flip back and jot reminders to <u>yourself on several days</u> prior to the deadline that you should work on the project. (15) When you sit down to do your homework, later, check off each assignment as you complete it. (16) If you follow these steps, you are much less likely to find yourself with your back against the wall at the last minute.

(17) Procrastination can get in the way of more than schoolwork. (18) I'm not saying that dreamers should stop <u>dreaming, but theres a time</u> for dreaming and a time for action.

(19) As a great <u>humanitarian named Dr. Albert Schweitzer once said, "dreams</u> will never become reality unless the dreamer faces reality moment by moment."

6   In sentence 12, how would <u>due, flip to the deadline date in you're</u> be correctly written?

F   do, flip to the deadline date in you're

G   due, flip to the deadline date in your

H   due flip to the deadline date in you're

J   As it is

7   In sentence 14, how would <u>yourself on several days</u> be correctly written?

A   yourself on severel days

B   yourselves on several days

C   oneself on several days

D   As it is

8   In sentence 18, how would <u>dreaming, but theres</u> be correctly written?

F   dreaming, but there's

G   dreaming but theres

H   dreaming, but there are

J   As it is

9   In sentence 19, how would <u>humanitarian named Dr. Albert Schweitzer once said, "dreams</u> be correctly written?

A   humanitarian, named Dr. Albert Schweitzer, once said, "dreams

B   humanitarian named Dr. Albert Schweitzer once said, "Dreams

C   humanitarian named dr. Albert Schweitzer once said, "dreams

D   As it is

Go On

208   Roadmap to the Virginia SOL: EOC English: Writing

Adam's teacher has asked students to write about what they learned while doing volunteer work. Before writing his essay, Adam made the following graphic organizer. Use it to answer question 10.

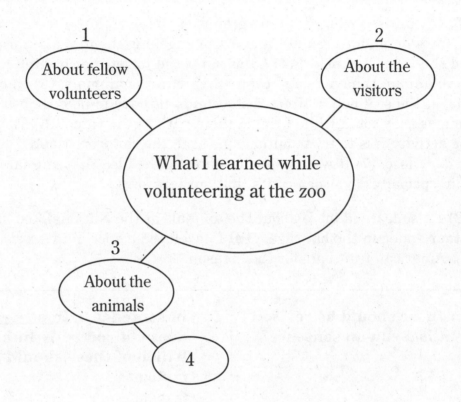

10 **Which of these belongs in bubble 4 in Adam's outline?**

F Many children are afraid of the dark when they go into the bat room.

G Many parents who don't know the answers to their kids' questions about bats make up the answers.

H Fruit bats especially enjoy eating bananas tied to the ceiling.

J Some volunteers take their jobs more seriously than others.

Go On

Here is the first part of Adam's rough draft. Use it to answer questions 11–14.

(1) I chose to volunteer at the National Zoo this summer. (2) My two months at the zoo taught me a lot about people as well as animals.

(3) My duties included taking groups of young children from various day camps on a tour around the zoo and engaging them in a program called the "Zoo Olympiad." (4) I was supposed to get the children to observe animal behaviors and competing with the animals. (5) <u>In other words,</u> at the seal pen, I directed the children to try to hold their breath as long as they could while I timed them with a stopwatch. (6) The goal of the activity was to try to outlast the seal, the children would invariably lose. (7) It was meant to reinforce the idea that animals have certain specially developed traits that surpass ours.

(8) I also learned more about the animals at the National Zoo. (9) The tour ended in the bat cage. (10) I developed a special interest in South American fruit bats for that reason.

11 Which of these should be revised because it is a run-on sentence?

   A 1

   B 4

   C 6

   D 7

12 In sentence 5, <u>In other words,</u> does *not* correctly link ideas. Which of these should be used instead?

   F However,

   G For example,

   H Although

   J Somehow,

Go On

13 Which is the *best* revision of sentence 4?

    A I was supposed to get the children to observe animal behaviors and they were supposed to compete with the animals.

    B I was supposed to get the children to observe animal behaviors. They were supposed to compete with the animals.

    C I was supposed to get the children to observe animal behaviors, they were supposed to compete with the animals.

    D I was supposed to get the children to observe animal behaviors and compete with the animals.

14 How can sentences 9 and 10 *best* be combined?

    F Because the tour ended in the bat cage, I developed a special interest in South American fruit bats.

    G The tour ended in the bat cage, therefore I developed a special interest in South American fruit bats.

    H The tour ended in the bat cage because I developed a special interest in South American fruit bats.

    J I developed a special interest in South American fruit bats so the tour ended in the bat cage.

Go On

Read this next section of Adam's rough draft and answer questions 15–18. This section has groups of underlined words. The questions ask about these groups of underlined words.

(11) Somehow bats have gotten a bad reputation they don't deserve. (12) Despite the common image of bats as bloodsuckers, fruit bats <u>eat only fruit and wouldn't never</u> endanger a person. (13) It was surprising to me that out of all the animals we saw at the zoo, these were the ones of which the children were most afraid. (14) <u>The bats is fed in an unusual</u> way. (15) Whole fruits such as <u>bunches of bananas, halved apples, and melon sections are hung</u> from the ceiling by a string. (16) The bats fly around and land on the fruit of their choice. (17) <u>Nestled inside musk melons, I was always amused to see small bats</u> munching happily away whenever we entered the bat house.

15 In sentence 12, how would <u>eat only fruit and wouldn't never</u> be correctly written?

A eat only fruit and would never

B ate only fruit and wouldn't never

C will eat only fruit and wouldn't never

D As it is

16 In sentence 14, how would <u>The bats is fed in an unusual</u> be correctly written?

F The bats are feeded in an unusual

G The bats are fed in an unusual

H The bats is fed in an unusaul

J As it is

17 In sentence 15, how would <u>bunches of bananas, halved apples, and melon sections are hung</u> be correctly written?

A bunches of bananas halved apples and melon sections are hung

B bunchs of bananas, halved apples, and melon sections are hung

C bunches of bananas, halved apples, and melon sections, are hung

D As it is

18 In sentence 17, how would <u>Nestled inside musk melons, I was always amused to see small bats</u> be correctly written?

F Nestled inside musk melons, it was always amusing to see small bats

G Nestled inside musk melons, I am always amused to see small bats

H I was always amused to see small bats nestled inside musk melons,

J As it is

Go On

Jorge's biology teacher has assigned a paper on endangered species. Jorge decides to contact the Nature Conservancy Center located near his home and request information on the work that is done there.

Jorge has begun a basic chart to focus his letter of request. Use it to answer question 19.

1. Who I am

2. What I need

3. Why I want it

4. When I need it

5. Where to send it

6. How I will use it

19 Which of these details belongs under number 2?

A science student at Wolf Trap High School

B information about research at the center on black-footed ferrets

C teacher has assigned paper on wildlife conservation

D deadline is January 25

Go On

Here is the first part of Jorge's rough draft. Use it to answer questions 20–23.

1743 Blake Street
Wolf Trap, Virginia 24592
December 3, 2000
Director
Nature Conservancy Center
PO Box 2640
Timberlake, Virginia 24502

Dear Director:

(1) I am a high school junior and I go to Wolf Trap High School. (2) I am writing to ask your help because I am supposed to write a report on endangered species for my science teacher. (3) I would especially appreciate any stuff you have on the black-footed ferret.

20 **Which is the *best* revision of sentence 1?**

F At Wolf Trap High School, I am a high school junior.

G I am a high school junior, I go to Wolf Trap High School.

H I am a junior in high school and I go to Wolf Trap High School.

J I am a junior at Wolf Trap High School.

21 **In writing this paragraph, Jorge *most* likely tried to —**

A capture the reader's attention with an interesting anecdote

B write with a humorous tone that would make the reader want to help

C clearly explain his identity and the purpose of his letter

D persuade the reader that the black-footed ferret is an endangered species

Go On

22 Which is the *best* revision of sentence 2?

    F I am writing to ask your help because my science teacher has assigned a report on endangered species.

    G My science teacher has assigned a report on endangered species and I am writing to ask your help.

    H To ask your help, I am writing to you because I am supposed to write a report on endangered species for my science teacher.

    J Because I am supposed to write a report on endangered species for my science teacher. I am writing to ask your help.

23 Which is the *best* revision of sentence 3?

    A I would especially appreciate any current information you have on the black-footed ferret.

    B I would especially appreciate anything at all you have on the black-footed ferret.

    C I would especially appreciate anything significant you have on the black-footed ferret.

    D I would especially appreciate anything interesting you have on the black-footed ferret.

Go On

Read this next section of Jorge's rough draft and answer questions 24–27. This section has groups of underlined words. The questions ask about these groups of underlined words.

(4) <u>There are less resources</u> on this endangered ferret than I had hoped! (5) <u>I am particular interested in the following kinds of information:</u>

(6) What is the history of this ferret in Virginia?

(7) Why is this ferret endangered?

(8) At your research center, <u>what research on this ferret is you presently doing?</u>

(9) What effort are you making to save this ferret?

(10) Do you have a bibliography and list of Web sites that I might find useful?

(11) Thank you in advance for your help. (12) <u>My paper is due on january 25,</u> so the sooner I get a response from you, the better. Sincerely,

Jorge Carreon

Jorge Carreon

---

24 In sentence 4, how would <u>**There are less**</u> resources be correctly written?

F There are fewer resources

G There is less resources

H There are less resource's

J As it is

25 In sentence 5, how would <u>**I am particular interested in the following kinds of information:**</u> be correctly written?

A I was particular interested in the following kinds of information:

B I was particular interested in the following kinds of information;

C I am particularly interested in the following kinds of information:

D As it is

26 In sentence 8, how would <u>what research on this ferret is you presently doing?</u> be correctly written?

   F what research, on this ferret, are you presently doing?

   G what research on this ferret were you presently doing?

   H what research on this ferret is you presently doing?

   J As it is

27 In sentence 12, how would <u>My paper is due on january 25,</u> be correctly written?

   A My paper was due on january 25,

   B My paper is due on January 25,

   C My paper is do on january 25,

   D As it is

Go On

Jackie is writing to a clothing company to complain about a hat that she bought at a school fund-raiser.

Jackie has created a basic outline to focus her ideas. Use it to answer question 28.

    I. Describe product

    II. Actions already taken

    III. Suggested action

28 **Which of these belongs under heading I in Jackie's outline?**

F I bought the baseball cap at a school fund-raiser.

G I told the parent in charge of the fund-raiser.

H The seam between visor and cap unraveled after being worn only once.

J I would like a cap to replace the one I'm returning.

Go On

Here is the first part of Jackie's draft. Use it to answer questions 29–32.

276 Blueridge Avenue
Veryfine, Virginia 20854
March 11, 2001
Customer Service Manager
School Fund-Raisers
PO Box 2673
New York, New York 10012

Dear Customer Service Manager:

(1) At the beginning of the school year, I ordered a baseball cap from your company. (2) I placed the order through a fund-raiser sponsored by our school's athletic department. (3) I received the cap I was pleased by the fit. (4) However, I am disappointed by the fact that it fell apart after I wore it only once. (5) I also think the hat would look better if you made the logo larger and more colorful.

(6) I put the cap on one Saturday morning and headed off to go shopping at the mall. (7) Later that day, the cap was worn while watching a friend's soccer game. (8) When I took the cap off after the game, I noticed that the seam had split between the cap and visor.

(9) I showed the cap to the parent in charge of the fund-raiser. (10) She suggested that I return the cap to you along with the receipt and a letter detailing what had happened.

Go On

29 **How can sentences 1 and 2 *best* be combined?**

A At the beginning of the school year, I ordered a baseball cap from your company, and I placed the order through a fund-raiser sponsored by our school's athletic department.

B At the beginning of the school year, I ordered a baseball cap from your company through a fund-raiser sponsored by our school's athletic department.

C At the beginning of the school year, I ordered a baseball cap from your company, I placed the order through a fund-raiser sponsored by our school's athletic department.

D I placed an order with your company through a fund-raiser sponsored by our school's athletic department at the beginning of the school year I ordered a baseball cap.

30 **How is sentence 3 *best* rewritten?**

F I received the cap, I was pleased by the fit.

G The cap was received and I was pleased by the fit.

H When I received the cap, I was pleased by the fit.

J I received and was pleased by the fit of the cap.

31 **Which sentence contains information that is *least* relevant to Jackie's letter?**

A 1

B 3

C 4

D 5

32 **Which is the *best* revision of sentence 7?**

F Later that day, I wore the cap while watching a friend's soccer game.

G Later that day, the cap was worn. I was watching a friend's soccer game.

H While watching a friend's soccer game, the cap was worn later that day.

J Later that day, the cap was worn. While watching a friend's soccer game.

Go On

Roadmap to the Virginia SOL: EOC English: Writing

Read this next section of Jackie's rough draft and answer questions 33–36. This section has groups of underlined words. The questions ask about these groups of underlined words.

(11) When you read my letter, <u>I'm sure that you will accept my story</u> and agree that I did not subject the cap to undue stress. (12) I'm also confident that once you examine the cap, <u>you'll send me a replacement cap with more sturdier</u> stitching. (13) I would appreciate your sending the new cap as soon as you can because <u>my friends and me plan to wear our caps on a trip to Seven Banners Amusement Park over spring</u> break.

(14) <u>Sincerely</u>

Jackie Jankovic

Jackie Jankovic

33 In sentence 11, how would <u>I'm sure that you will accept my story</u> be correctly written?

A Im sure that you will accept my story

B I'm sure that you'd accept my story.

C I'm sure that you will except my story

D As it is

34 In sentence 12, how would <u>you'll send me a replacement cap with more sturdier</u> be correctly written?

F yo'ull send me a replacement cap with more sturdier

G you'll send me a replacement cap with sturdier

H you'd send me a replacement cap with more sturdier

J As it is

Go On

35 In sentence 13, how would <u>my friends and me plan to wear our caps on a trip to Seven Banners Amusement Park over spring</u> be correctly written?

   A my friends and I plan to wear our caps on a trip to Seven Banners Amusement Park over spring

   B my friends and me plan to wear our caps on a trip to Seven Banners amusement park over spring

   C my friends and me plan to wear out caps on a trip to Seven Banners Amusement Park over Spring

   D As it is

36 In line 14, how would <u>Sincerely</u> be correctly written?

   F sincerely

   G Sincerly

   H Sincerely,

   J As it is

Devarn has been asked by his art teacher to write a short biography of his favorite artist, Diego Rivera. The biography will be displayed at the mall during Arts in the Schools Week.

Devarn made this chart to organize the facts on his index cards. Use it to answer question 37.

Diego Rivera	Facts
Early Years	(1) Born in Guanajuato, Mexico, 1886
	(2) Began study at School of Fine Arts at age 10
Middle Years success	(3) First exhibit, 1905—a great
	(4) Influence of cubism on his colorful painting, 1912–1913
	(5) Married artist Frida Kahlo, 1929
Later Years	(6)
	(7) Died in 1957

37 **Which of these facts should Devarn write beside 6 on the chart?**

A Painted most famous mural, Sunday Dream, 1947

B Diego sent to live in the country after his two-year-old twin dies

C When young studied in carving workshop of artist José Guadalupe Posada

D At age 6, moved to Mexico City with his family

Go On

Below are two drafts of the first part of Devarn's biography. Use these two rough drafts to answer questions 38–40.

DRAFT A

Diego Rivera was born in the late 1800s. <u>He was born in Mexico. He had a brother, Carlos. He died when he was two.</u> Diego was sent to live in the mountains for a while. Diego's family moved a few years later.

Diego began to study at the School of Fine Arts in San Carlos at night. He went to regular school during the day. He studied in a carving workshop. The workshop was run by artist José Guadalupe Posada. Rivera had his first art exhibit in 1905. It was a great success. The government awarded him a trip to Europe. He met Pablo Picasso in Europe. Picasso's cubist style influenced Rivera's work. He married the famous painter Frida Kahlo in 1929.

DRAFT B

Diego Rivera, a famous muralist painter, was born in Guanajuato, Mexico, in 1886. His twin brother, Carlos, died when he was two. To protect Diego from illness, Diego's parents sent him to live in the mountains where the climate was healthier for four years. In 1892, the family moved to Mexico City.

Diego began to study at the School of Fine Arts in San Carlos at night while going to regular school during the day. He studied in the carving workshop of artist José Guadalupe Posada. Then, in 1905, he had his first art exhibit. It was such a success that the government awarded him with a trip to Europe. There he met Pablo Picasso, whose cubist style influenced Rivera's work. In 1929, he married Frida Kahlo. She was a famous artist who began painting while recovering from a bus accident at age 18. The vividness of her paintings and her colorful, traditional costumes were both influenced by Mexican folk culture.

38 Which draft contains information that is off the topic?

   F Draft A, because it tells about Rivera's studying art at night school

   G Draft B, because it tells that Frida Kahlo's painting and dress were colorful

   H Draft A, because it describes the influence that Picasso had on Rivera's work

   J Draft B, because it tells about Rivera's first art exhibit

39 The first sentence of Draft B is more effective than the first sentence of Draft A because it —

   A shifts the point of view for emphasis

   B provides more specific detail

   C makes a direct, persuasive appeal to the reader

   D contains highly technical language

40 <u>He was born in Mexico. He had a brother, Carlos. He died when he was two.</u> In paragraph 1 of Draft A, which of these is a problem with these sentences?

   F They express Devarn's personal opinion about Diego Rivera.

   G They should be moved to the end of the paragraph.

   H They have a choppy rhythm because sentence beginnings and types are not varied.

   J They are off the topic of Devarn's biography of Diego Rivera.

Go On

Read this next section of Devarn's rough draft and answer questions 41–44. This section has groups of underlined words. The questions ask about these groups of underlined words.

He took his art to the public by painting colorful, realistic murals in the streets and on buildings. He captured important moments in Mexican history, he used his work for social commentary. His works often show images of the earth the farmer, and the laborer. Two of his most famous pieces are the fresco at the Palace of Fine Arts and his famous mural, Sunday dream, in the Hotel del Prado. He worked right up until his death in 1957, two years after his wife's passing.

41 How would Mexican history, he be correctly written?

A mexican history, he

B Mexican history, and he

C Mexican History, he

D As it is

42 How would the earth the farmer, and the laborer be correctly written?

F the earth, the farmer, and the laborer

G the Earth the farmer, and the laborer

H the earth the farmer, and laboring

J As it is

43 How would Palace of Fine Arts and his famous mural, Sunday dream, be correctly written?

A palace of Fine Arts and his famous mural, Sunday dream,

B Palace of Fine Arts and his famous mural, sunday dream,

C Palace of Fine Arts and his famous mural, Sunday Dream,

D As it is

44 How would two years after his wife's be correctly written?

F   too years after his wife's

G two year's after his wife's

H two years after his wives

J As it is

Go On

WRITING PROMPT

What do you think of the idea that the minimum driving age should be raised to 18? Write an opinion piece for your school newspaper. Support your position with reasons and examples.

Writing Checklist

___ Did I plan and organize the paper before writing it?

Did I revise the paper to include

    ___ an attention-getting introduction?

    ___ plenty of specific, supporting evidence for the central idea?

    ___ only ideas that support that main idea?

    ___ sentences and paragraphs that follow a logical order?

    ___ sentences that are clear, varied, and smooth flowing?

    ___ vocabulary that conveys a tone appropriate for my audience and purpose?

    ___ a conclusion that offers a wrap-up without just saying the same thing again?

Did I edit the paper to make sure that

    ___ grammar is correct?

    ___ capitalization is correct?

    ___ fragments and run-ons are eliminated?

    ___ misplaced modifiers are put in the right place?

    ___ spelling is error-free?

Did I go over the paper to ensure that

    ___ my purpose in writing the paper is clearly communicated?

    ___ the paper accomplishes what it is supposed to?

Go On ⇒

Go On

Go On

ANSWERS AND EXPLANATIONS FOR PRACTICE EXAM 2

ANSWERS AND EXPLANATIONS
FOR PRACTICE EXAM 2

ANSWER KEY

Multiple Choice

1 A When you're giving step-by-step instructions, it makes sense to put the steps in time order, right? Fiona is suggesting steps a student might take to keep homework under control by using an assignment book. So far, she has walked the student through steps to take during the school day: jot down assignments, note deadlines, etc. The next logical step, time-wise, comes when the student finally does the assignment: Check it off! **(A)** Eliminate **B, C,** and **D** because, while they might be good general suggestions, they don't fit next in the time sequence for this specific task—keeping an assignment notebook.

2 G Fiona's first paragraph isn't especially attention-grabbing, so eliminate **F.** She also isn't explaining how to avoid procrastination—she does that in the second paragraph—so eliminate **J.** She is not at all criticizing the reader **(H);** in fact, her tone is very reassuring ("I'm sure your letter rang a bell...," "It's not uncommon...," "I'm glad that you wrote...").

3 D Remember how to find fragments (incomplete sentences)? Check for "sentences" that are missing either a subject or verb (or both) and can't stand alone. Sentence 8 is missing both. The reader is left to wonder: Who (subject) does what (verb) when your teacher gives these assignments?

4 H These are two complete ideas, each with its own subject and verb. "There are some simple steps you can take" can stand alone as a sentence and so can "these steps can help you manage your time for doing homework."

5 A The word "invest" is the only precise one, here, and it suggests a particular act—buying. Vague, anemic words, like "get" and "take," are overused and don't say much.

6 G Watch out for commonly confused words such as *your* and *you're. You're* going to get *your* diploma. Chuck any choices that add new problems not in the original. **F** uses the wrong "do": Whatever you *do,* return your books before they're *due.* **H** omits a necessary comma after an introductory phrase ("As soon as you learn when a long-term project is due").

7 **D** The pronoun "yourself" agrees with its singular antecedent "you."

8 **F** Don't forget to throw in an apostrophe to take the place of the letter(s) missing from a contraction.

9 **B** When punctuating dialogue, remember to capitalize the first word of an exact quote. Here, you can use POE to get rid of **A**, **C**, and **D** because they don't fix the original problem ("dreams...").

10 **H** Fruit bats are animals, so they go after the about-the-animals bubble (4). Reject **F** and **G** because children and parents would go in the visitors' bubble (2). Forget **J** because it belongs in the fellow volunteers' bubble (1).

11 **C** These are two complete ideas, each with its own subject and verb. "The goal of the activity was to try to outlast the seal" can stand alone as a sentence and so can "The children would invariably lose." Neither leaves the reader dangling, wondering "Who?" or "Does what?"

12 **G** Sentence 5 (about the hold-your-breath game) is an illustration. It shows what the Zoo Olympiad, introduced in the sentence before, was like. Therefore, it is best linked by the phrase, "For example,".

13 **D** Remember to trim the fat wherever possible. The only sentence that gets rid of the repeated phrase "supposed to" is **D**.

14 **F** Only **F** suggests the intended cause-and-effect relationship. The result of ending up every day in the bat cage was that he got especially interested in the bats. Eliminate **G** because it contains a new error: When you use "therefore" to connect two complete ideas, you need a semicolon (;) and not a comma to link the ideas. **H** doesn't work because the meaning is turned on its head. The special interest in bats was an effect that resulted *after* frequent stops in the bat house on the tour, not a cause of those stops.

15 **A** Beware the double negative. ("Wouldn't" is already negative, so you don't need another negative word, "never.") Once you spot this big double-negative mistake, you don't need to examine the choices carefully. Just spot the one that corrects the error.

16 **G** Remember: Verbs Are Ticklish: Verbs must agree with their subjects and be the right tense. Here, the plural subject (bats) requires a plural verb (are). That eliminates **H** and **J**. **F** is no-go because *feed* is one of those irregular verbs you have to memorize. (There is no such word as "feeded," although there would be if words stuck to the past tense spelling rule!)

17 **D** This is fine as-is because the writer remembered to *separate* items in a series with commas. **B** almost works—but the writer forgot that rule about adding -*es* to form the plural of words that end in *x* or *ch*. **C** almost works—but there is an extra comma after the *last* item in the series (where it does *not* belong).

18 **H** This is one of those silly misplaced modifiers. The way it's written, the sentence makes you picture Adam curled up in a melon! Who or what is nestled in those melons? Not "it" (choice **F**) and not "I" (choices **G** and **J**). Remember to keep the describing phrase nice and close to what it describes.

19 **B** You can use the 5 Ws and 1 H to organize ideas for all sorts of writing—especially business letters. The info on ferrets is *what* you need, so that goes in the "What?" box. Choice **A** would go in the "Who?" box, choice **C** would go in the "Why?" box and choice **D** belongs in the "When?" box.

20 **J** Use POE to eliminate **F** because the word order just sounds awkward, plus the phrase "high school" is repeated unnecessarily. Choice **G** goes out the window because it is a faulty comma splice (that incorrectly links two complete ideas). Choice **H** is wordier than **J**, and therefore not as strong a choice.

21 **C** The opener does what it is supposed to do—makes the author's identity and purpose clear—so eliminate **B** and **D**. Some writers do use an anecdote to grab their readers' attention—but not this one; eliminate **A**.

22 **G** There is nothing technically wrong with **F**, but it doesn't correct the choppy rhythm of the sentences in the first paragraph, most of which begin the same way, with "I" ("I am...," "I am...," "I would..."). **H** puts words in a weird order and sounds awkward. Toss **J** immediately because it contains a fragment. The first "sentence" (Because...teacher.) is an incomplete idea that leaves the reader wondering, "Who does what because of that?"

23 **A** The word "anything" is about as vague and unacceptable as "stuff," but "current information" does the trick by telling precisely what Adam wants.

24 **F** Remember the less/fewer rule. If you can count'em, use "fewer."

25 **C** Remember how snooty adjectives like "particular" are? They only describe nouns, not adjectives like "interested." Adverbs (usually ending in -*ly*) describe verbs and adjectives, so you need "particularly," here. Give **B** the boot because it substitutes a semicolon when the colon is just fine where it is (signaling, "as follows").

26 **J** There's nothing wrong with this (and remember, about one-fourth of the time "as it is" will be the right answer), but you can use POE to knock down each of the choices. The commas in **F** are unnecessary. (The phrase "on this ferret" is essential because you don't want to know about all research, so *don't* set off the phrase with commas. Only set off interrupting, unnecessary phrases.) Cross off **G** because the word "presently" clues you in to the fact that you need a present tense verb (*are*, not *were*).

27 **B** *Always* capitalize the names of months. Because only one choice corrects this error, you can skip over the others!

28 **H** Choice **H** is the only one that describes the faulty product—a cap that fell apart. Choice **G** would go under heading II, because it has to do with a past action. Choice **J** would go under heading III, because it expresses the writer's suggestion about what the company should do.

29 **B** Be leery of long, windy choices like **A** that simply slap two ideas together with the word "and." They're technically okay, but not graceful and concise. **C** is downright wrong (a comma splice) and so is **D** (a fused sentence, or "run-on").

30 **H** Choice **H** makes nice use of the transition word, "When" to show the relationship between the two ideas in the sentence. Use POE to get rid of **F** (a comma splice). Choice **G** sounds awkward because it incorrectly throws the passive tense into a letter that has been written in the active voice, so far. Choice **J** is weak, too, because of the awkward, unparallel wording.

31 **D** Jackie wrote the letter for one purpose—to get a new cap—and all sentences in the letter should help accomplish that purpose. How she would improve the logo has nothing to do with getting an exchange on a faulty cap.

32 **F** This choice is the only one that corrects the problem with passive voice (the cap was worn). There is rarely a good reason to use the passive voice in a letter like this. Instead, be assertive, use active verbs, and get to the point! Not only does **J** fail to correct the passive voice error, but it adds a new one: "While watching a friend's soccer game" is a fragment.

33 **D** The original is fine, but check for common errors anyway. Choice **A** adds one common mistake—forgetting the apostrophe in a contraction ("I'm"). Choice **B** shifts tense for no reason ("you'd" instead of "you will"). Choice **C** contains another common slip—"except" instead of "accept." Remember: I will *accept* any excuse *except* that one.

34 **G** Be careful with comparative forms of adjectives and adverbs. This one is sturdy. That one is sturdier. You don't need *more* because "sturdier" already means "more sturdy."

35 **A** Focus on what's wrong with the sentence. There's nothing wrong with the capitalization. The name of an amusement park is capitalized and the general name of a season (spring) is not. Whenever you see a pair of people like "my sister and I" or "my friends and me" in a sentence, check the pronoun. Remember how? Split up those people! My friends plan to wear...I plan to wear.

36 **H** This is one of those simple conventions you need to brand into your brain. Commas belong in certain places whenever you write a letter: in dates, addresses (between city and state), and after the close ("Sincerely,").

37 **A** Since points 6 and 7 come in the "Later Years" block, they should tell about the artist's later life. Choices **B** and **D** won't work, because they tell about Diego Rivera's childhood and choice **C** is out, too, because it describes his young adulthood.

38 **G** The purpose of Devarn's biography is to describe the life and work of Rivera, and all sentences in the composition should do that. The fact that Rivera married Kahlo is relevant, but the description of her painting and dress goes off on a tangent.

39 **B** You can tell right away that the first sentence of Draft B is longer than the first sentence of Draft A. What might make a sentence longer and better than another? Not **A** or **C**, and **D** would rarely make a sentence better. In fact, the first sentence of Draft B provides more specific information than the first *two* sentences of Draft A.

40 **H** These sentences are factual, not Devarn's opinion, and they are about Diego Rivera's life, so eliminate choices **F** and **J**. They describe events early in Rivera's life, so eliminate choice **G**. But all three sentences are short and begin with "He."

41 **B** Beware the comma splice! If the ideas on either side of the comma can each stand alone (as they can, here), you need more than a comma to separate them!

42 **F** Separate *all* the items in a series with commas. Eliminate **G** because you only capitalize "Earth" when you are referring to the name of the planet. Get rid of **H** because there is a parallelism problem. These are three similar ideas (things depicted by the painter), so express them in a similar way: earth, farmer, laborer.

43 **C** Capitalize titles of works like novels and paintings. You can use POE to cross off **A** because it doesn't capitalize the proper name of a place (Palace of Fine Arts) and **B** because it fails to capitalize both words in the title of Rivera's mural.

44 **J** Don't mix up the three words, *to*, *too*, and *two* (as choice **F** mistakenly does). Also, don't confuse possessives (where you often need apostrophes) with plurals (where you don't). That's the mistake that choice **G** ("two year's") makes. Finally, knock out choice **H** because Devarn is talking about the death of one wife (singular, possessive), and "wives" is plural.

ESSAY

What do you think of the idea that the minimum driving age should be raised to 18? Write an opinion piece for your school newspaper. Support your position with reasons and examples.

Sample Essay A: A Barely Passing Essay

Our two fictional scorers each gave this an 8 for a total of 16 points.

I am against rasing the age for getting a driver's license to 18. Here's why:

Although many drivers have accidents the first year they drive. It isn't just because they are a young age. It is true that by stastistics a 16 year old is nine times more probable to get into a driving accident than an older driver. However, being a teenager is not the reason that teens has more acidents than others, inexperience is. The result of increasing the driving age to 18 would just be to have 18 year olds causing most of acidents. Getting driving experience takes time, years in fact, it ca'nt be rushed.

The motor vehical adminsteration reports that the greatest time collision rates goes down are when drivers is between 20 and 24 years old. The reason for this trend is because it take about four to eight years to get enough driving experiance. It don't make no sense to push up the driving age to 18. That would just mean inexperienced drivers was on the road a couple of years later. Actally a 18 year old could be more careless than a teenaged driver who is still under their parents supervision. Parents of a 16 year old first have to teach their child driving skills and then monitor his or her driving. Even those 18 year olds who still live at home, they is less likely to have they parents try to restrict and hold back driving privileges. On the other hand, parents can have they underage child's license yanked. Most teenagers wants to drive as soon as they can. If the minimum driving age is rased, the result would be pretty wild. Seventeen year olds would be running out for permits. Many of them will ask a little older friends for driving lessons. These friends are pretty weak drivers themself. Would you like the ones running out for permits to be 18 year olds. Would you rather have them be 15 year olds which is more likely to have a parent around to teach him to drive?

It takes alot to drive. it takes education, skill, and being perseverent. If the driving age is raised to 18, accidents will probably increase. Most sixteen year olds have something going for them. Its something that many 18 year olds do not. they are still under their parents wings. Who teach them driving skills they themself learned through long experience. Adult 18 year olds, on the other hand, is not protected by parents as much. They also don't have to find a good driving teacher. Its a bad idea to make it so the new drivers are also the ones that are just starting to be new adults in the eyes of the Law.

Composing Domain: 3

Written Expression Domain: 3

Sentence Formation/Usage/Mechanics Domain: 2

This paper rates a 3 in the composing domain. The article's central idea—that the driving age should not be lowered—is purposefully elaborated, although rather thinly in the third paragraph. (For example, the writer could have improved his general statement about an 18 year old's being more careless than a younger driver by mentioning statistics kept by the Department of Transportation that support this claim. Likewise, the contention that parents' monitoring protects a younger teen would have been strengthened by an illustration—e.g., on a stormy night, parents can protect their 16 year old by denying permission for him to drive on rain-slicked roads.) There are occasional lapses in logic: "The result of increasing the driving age to 18 would just be to have 18 year olds causing most of accidents"? There are few digressions or point-of-view shifts and the piece has an opening and closing. However, it would need more elaboration and no organizational lapses to achieve a score of 4.

The paper's written expression domain is a 3. Specific vocabulary is present ("monitor," "restrict," "privileges"), but so is general vocabulary ("want," "pretty wild," "pretty weak," "bad idea").

In the sentence formation/usage/mechanics domain, this student earns a 2 for inconsistent control of the domain's features. There are several fragments ("Although many drivers have accidents ...," "Who teach them driving skills ..."), severe errors in grammar ("teens has," "It don't make sense," "themself"), many errors in spelling, punctuation, and capitalization (e.g., "motor vehical adminsteration"). Paragraphs are not indented properly.

Sample Essay B: An Excellent Essay

This received a maximum score of 12 from each of our two fictional scorers for a total of 24.

I know that my position on keeping younger teens off the road is going to be unpopular, but here it is: Sixteen is often too young to drive. Recent research suggests that 16 year olds are simply too young to be handed the car keys. Among 15 to 20 year olds, motor vehicle accidents are the leading cause of death, according to statistics kept by the National Highway Traffic Safety Administration. In 1997 alone, 3,336 teens between ages 15 and 20 were killed on the roads and 365,000 were injured.

The Insurance Institute for Highway Safety reports that for drivers aged 16-19, the risk of being involved in a crash is four times the risk for older drivers. An expert in adolescent medicine at Children's National Medical Center in the nation's capital was recently quoted in the Washington Post as saying that age 16 is probably the worst time in an adolescent's life to accept the responsibility for driving. He supports this assertion by pointing out that teens have underdeveloped motor skills that cause them to react more slowly than young adults who are a few years older.

In addition to having less-developed motor skills, a 16 year old may have less than adequate decision-making skills. The IIHS concludes that teens have higher collision rates mainly because of inexperience and immaturity, particularly when it comes to risky driving practices like speeding and tailgating. According to the IIHS, most crashes involving young drivers are single-car crashes, mainly crashes involving driver error and speeding that result in going off the road.

Sixteen-year-olds are also notoriously distractable, sociable, and emotional. Add to this mix a common sense of invincibility and a typical result is risky behavior.

In other words, if you put a 16 year old behind the wheel in a car full of teenage passengers, you are asking for trouble.

Of course inexperience and distractability will hinder any new driver, regardless of his or her age. However, the older the driver, the higher his or her maturity level will usually be. If new drivers had to *wait until 18 to get their licenses, these new drivers would have judgment and decision-making skills that would be better developed. They would be less likely to engage in risky driving behavior, which would result, in turn, in fewer accidents.*

The mere fact that 16 has always been the minimum driving age is no excuse for keeping it that way. Increasing the driving age to 18 would protect more people than recklessly continuing to allow 16 year olds to get licenses. Teenagers have been getting on with their lives for 16 years without a license. Waiting one or two more years will not kill them, and it may mean saving their lives.

Composing Domain: 4

Written Expression Domain: 4

Sentence Formation/Usage/Mechanics Domain: 4

This paper receives a 4 in the composing domain. The central idea—the writer's position in support of raising the driving age—is sharply focused and fully elaborated. She presents ample detail in support of her position, including NHTSA statistics, expert quotes, and IIHS conclusions. Organization is strong, with careful application of logic as she systematically builds her case with reasons (a 16 year old's motor-skills, decision-making skills, distractibility, etc.).

This paper also scores a 4 in the written expression domain. Point of view is consistent, with no digressions. There is consistent control of vocabulary (precise word choice like "assertion" and "invincibility"), even presentation of information, strong voice, and a purposeful tone. There are only one or two awkward sentence constructions (e.g., "If new drivers had to wait until 18 to get their licenses, these new drivers would have judgment and decision-making skills that would be better developed."). Overall, the rhythm is smooth and effective due to a variety of sentence beginnings, lengths, and types.

Finally, the paper scores a 4 in the sentence formation/usage/mechanics domain. All features of this domain are correctly intact. The only two surface errors are the misspellings of "distractability" and "adequite."

The Princeton Review

Partnering with You to Measurably Improve Student Achievement

Our proven 3-step approach lets you **assess** student performance, **analyze** the results, and **act** to improve every student's mastery of skills covered by the Virginia Standards of Learning.

Assess
Deliver formative and benchmark tests

Analyze
Review in-depth performance reports and implement ongoing professional development

Act
Utilize after school programs, course materials, and enrichment resources

Order Roadmap books for your classroom or school.

II 1-800-REVIEW-2 • E-mail K12sales@review.com • Visit educators.princetonreview.com

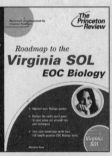
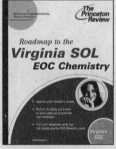